The Teen's Guide to Social Skills

The TEEN'S GUIDE

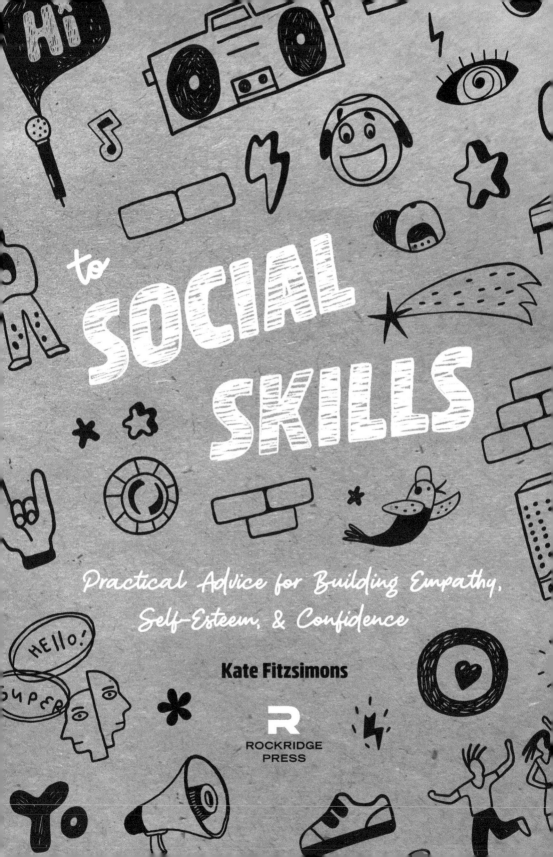

to SOCIAL SKILLS

Practical Advice for Building Empathy,
Self-Esteem, & Confidence

Kate Fitzsimons

ROCKRIDGE PRESS

To my big sister and social butterfly, Nicole.

Interior and Cover Designer: Gabe Nansen
Art Producer: Sue Bischofberger
Editors: Meera Pal, Barbara J. Isenberg
Production Editor: Nora Milman
All illustrations used under license from iStock.com and Shutterstock.com
Author photo courtesy of Princeton Headshots

ISBN: Print 978-1-64876-617-6 | eBook 978-1-64876-116-4

R0

Contents

Introduction

You know those people who can walk into a party and everyone seems to gravitate toward them? They're outgoing, friendly, and always know what to say to strike up a good conversation with anyone. I'm not one of those people—and neither are most of the teens I coach. Yes, that's right, I coach teens on self-confidence and social skills because, for many people, those things don't come naturally.

Despite being a high achiever with a supportive family, I struggled as a teen. I had difficulty coping with the emotional turmoil of friendship challenges, the pressure to study, and social expectations. I avoided trying new activities and going to new places. Small talk with strangers was my greatest fear because I never knew what to say. Perhaps the worst part was the unrealistic expectations I put on myself and the self-loathing that followed. My anxiety and shame caused emotional meltdowns that hurt the ones I loved most.

My wake-up call came in 2012 when my beautiful older sister, Nicole, was killed in an accident overseas. I was shattered by the grief and despair of losing her. But it also reminded me to stop taking my life for granted.

I was sick of being the anxious, anorexic girl crying herself to sleep.

I was sick of worrying about what my friends thought about me.

I was sick of the negative voice telling me to hide away.

I was sick of taking my self-loathing out on my family by lashing out at them.

Honestly, I was sick of hating myself.

I realized that to change I had to learn how to take charge of my own emotions, become less anxious, and be more confident. I wanted to start living—for myself and my sister. Through putting in the hard work to improve my social skills, I was able to ditch the excuses and turn in my "victim card." By age 24, I had become a certified life coach with a mission to empower teens like you to become the resilient generation I know you can be.

If you can relate to these struggles, I'm so glad you're reading this book. This book is meant to be your guide on how to get past these challenges. Even if you don't think it's possible and you just are who you are, all I'm asking is for you to keep an open mind. Although being confident in social situations may not come naturally to you, it's something you can improve. This book will show you how, step-by-step.

I'm not here to lecture you, judge you, or tell you what to do. I'm here as your mentor and your coach to bring out the best in you. I'll teach you simple strategies you can use to better handle your emotions and connect with others, so you feel more confident no matter who you're around.

You may be younger than I am, but you are not below me. You are my peer, my fellow human who has fears, worries, and insecurities just like me. But I also know that just like me, you have the potential to stop letting those fears hold you back. It takes practice building these social skills, but I'm here to guide you every step of the way. I think you may be surprised at how much more you will get out of your life once you no longer fear or care about what others think.

So let's get started!

How to Use This Book

Before we really dive into social skills, I want to briefly explain how this book is laid out and why.

There isn't just one magical thing you need to fix to become less socially awkward. This process involves developing skills across a range of key areas. And to ensure I don't overload you with too much info all at once, we'll tackle one specific skill at a time. Each chapter opens with a scenario in which someone is lacking in one of the skills. I'll break down how it's affecting them and their relationships. (I'm sure you'll be able to relate to a few.) Then I'll take you through cool strategies to help you develop that skill and put it into practice so you can begin to change your social interactions for the better.

My goal is to make the book fun and easy to understand and to offer you strategies that are simple to remember. You are welcome to skip around, but the chapters are organized to help you build upon the previous skill. You'll improve your social skills the most if you read it all the way through.

It doesn't matter if your goal is to stop arguing with your parents, feel more confident around strangers, or make more friends at school. Nearly every area of your life involves interacting and communicating with people, so this book will help you develop the social skills you need to live your best life.

Yes, some areas may feel uncomfortable because it takes effort to push outside your comfort zone. But I don't want you to miss out on something amazing just because it feels difficult. The struggle is worth it. There's nothing that compares to feeling comfortable and confident in your own skin and being able to connect with others so they feel understood—and you do, too.

Keep on reading, knowing that your future self will thank you for it.

Chapter One

LET'S TALK SOCIAL SKILLS

One Christmas my then-boyfriend and I drove from New Jersey all the way down to Florida. The day before we left, I pulled up Google Maps and looked over the route we'd be taking and all the different terrain and places we'd pass through. That's what this chapter is—a road map of what we'll cover throughout this book. It'll establish the starting point of where you're at on this journey of growing your social skills and then give you an overview of all the different content we'll explore to get from where you are now to where you want to be.

THE ABCs OF SOCIAL SKILLS

So, here we are! You've ended up with this book in your hands because someone you know thinks it will be helpful for you to read it.

I know it can be annoying when adults tell us to do things. You may be thinking, *Why should I bother reading this book? There are so many other things I'd rather be doing in my spare time!* But let me take a moment to explain why this book is better than surfing YouTube for crazy cat videos or binge-watching Netflix. I know it's a big claim, but here's why I'm confident making it:

As happy as those things make you, I also know how awful that knot in your stomach feels when you're about to walk into a friend's party where you know no one else and your hands can't stop shaking. I also know how much anxiety you feel when you're paired up for a group assignment and you wish the ground would swallow you up because you hate speaking in front of others. None of those feelings of awkwardness are fun at all.

It's totally natural to feel nervous around people, especially people we don't know well. But you can stop letting anxiety get the better of you and build the confidence to put yourself out there in social situations.

The reality is that the older you get, the more often you're going to face these awkward scenarios of meeting and speaking with people from all walks of life. We live in a social world. That's why I believe this book is the best way to use your spare time. It's also why the adult in your life gave you this book. They care about you and they believe in you. And so do I.

With practice, I know you can develop these social skills. And I will be here to guide you with practical strategies every step of the way. Being socially awkward isn't a fixed trait like your eye color or nose shape. It's caused by habits, beliefs, traits, and tendencies that are flexible and changeable.

Maybe you suffer social anxiety because you think you're not cool enough. Or maybe your autism makes it challenging to hold eye contact with others. Or maybe you've always been called the shy one and find it hard to make friends. No matter the cause of your social awkwardness, this book will help you better understand it and improve upon it.

DEVELOPING SOCIAL SKILLS

Have you ever wondered why some people seem to have no problems chatting in large groups, while others seem to be at a loss for words and just look dazed and confused? The reason some of us struggle more when it comes to being comfortable in social situations isn't because there's something weird about us. It may simply be due to differences in our chemical makeup. Let's unpack this a little more by looking at some research that I promise won't bore you to tears.

Researchers from the National University of Singapore found that two distinct strands of DNA that regulate oxytocin (the "love hormone") can directly affect a person's natural abilities when it comes to social skills. Oxytocin is the chemical in our brain that's a big driver behind our social behavior, including connecting with others, feeling empathy, and building trust. People with lower levels of oxytocin may struggle a little more in these areas.

So if you don't naturally light up at the idea of going to hang out in a big group of friends at the mall, or you would rather eat your own sock than run for student council, it doesn't mean there's something wrong with you, and it's nothing to be ashamed of. It just means you're human. Each human being is uniquely different from the next, and that's what makes the world such an interesting place.

There's no need to compare how shy you are with how shy your friend or sibling is (or isn't). They're not ahead of or better than you if they find it easier to be social. Each of you just had different starting points on this journey of developing your social skills—and that's okay. Whether it's because you are low on oxytocin, have a condition like autism, or have high anxiety, this is just one part of what determines your social skills. It's all about adapting and calling upon your other abilities and resources.

The REWARDS

"But why, Dad?"

At this moment, getting off the couch to go to your brother's basketball game is the last thing you feel like doing. It's a cold night, you're warm and toasty in your hoodie, but most of all—there are going to be people from your grade there. Lots of them. Eh, it's just not your scene.

Does this scenario sound familiar? Sometimes it's much easier to hide away and not interact with your peers. It's usually a lot easier to play video games than make small talk with someone new. So why should we bother socializing with our peers at all?

Imagine if someone said to you, "Hey, I can help you live longer, have more meaningful friendships, be more resilient, less anxious, boost your confidence, improve your grades, make your transition into college life far more enjoyable, and set you up for a better career path." Would you be interested? I know I've got both of my hands up! And those are just a *few* of the benefits that can come from being more social.

Although it's tempting to become a hermit, your future self will thank you for improving your social skills now. In fact, researchers have found that having close friends during your teen years won't just make you happier now but will lead to less depression later in life.

As human beings, we are innately social. Connecting, interacting, and forming relationships is how we've grown and thrived as a species for so many years. That's why the benefits of being social expand across all areas of your life, for the rest of your life.

Developmental psychologist Susan Pinker notes that face-to-face contact releases neurotransmitters in our brains. "And like a vaccine, they protect you now in the present and well into the future." Her research has found that interacting in person with others boosts our levels of oxytocin and other important hormones that can help lower stress and anxiety.

You know that warm and fuzzy feeling you get after a deep and meaningful chat with someone you care about? That's what Susan Pinker is talking about.

THE FIVE Ws OF SOCIAL SKILLS

Now we're up to the part in our road map where I am going to break down the five Ws of social skills to help you better understand what social skills really are and how you can develop them.

The What

Two words you've seen me repeat many times already are *social skills*, but what do I really mean by that? Am I talking about saying, "please" and "thank you"? Or is it remembering not to stand too close to another person? Is it remembering to look someone in the eye and smile when they talk to you?

Well, it's really a combination of all of these and more. There are different variations on the same definition. This one from Kid Sense Child Development says, "Social skills are the skills we use every day to interact and communicate with others. They include verbal and nonverbal communication, such as speech, gesture, facial expression, and body language."

From paying attention to what someone is saying to uncrossing your arms and showing genuine care for how that person is feeling, social skills are the things we use to help people in our presence feel seen, heard, comfortable, and connected to us.

- *I see you.*   - *I hear you.*   - *I feel you.*

That's what social skills are to me. They are also the behaviors we use to make it easy for others to make *us* feel seen, heard, and comfortable. Those include actions like expressing ourselves clearly, speaking in an appropriate tone of voice, knowing how to ask thoughtful questions, and keeping a relaxed posture. It's all part of the process through which people better understand and show interest in each other.

As we know, this comes naturally for some people. For others, it's not so easy. If you've ever come across someone who seems standoffish, barely responds to your attempt at small talk, or looks away when you try explaining something to them, that person may be socially awkward. In fact, some of us *are* that person. But you can transition from being that awkward person who feels totally uncomfortable in social situations to someone who knows how to listen actively and participate naturally in conversations, so everyone feels engaged and connected.

If this doesn't come naturally to you, it doesn't mean you're flawed. It means that people who are more outgoing and make social skills look easy may have learned these strategies when they were younger or have a slightly different chemical makeup, as I explained earlier. We all have our unique strengths and weaknesses, so it's not fair to compare yourself to others. The only two people you should compare are:

1. The person you are right now.

2. The person you are becoming once you've learned and practiced these social-skills strategies.

You may see huge growth as you put these skills into practice. That's worth noticing and being proud of. Focus on that. As my coach often tells me, "Stay in your lane." It's how we progress the fastest.

The Why

It's the feeling of winning the basketball district championship with your team. Of having a friend wipe away his tears and thank you for cheering him up. Of getting the call from the local grocery store to say, "Congratulations, you've got your first job!"

All these moments can elicit those invaluable feelings of pride, satisfaction, and purpose. You know what else they have in common? They all involve a variety of social skills to make them happen. You don't get to be a part of a winning basketball team without learning how to interact with your teammates. You can't help a friend feel better without learning how to feel empathy for their emotions. You won't be hired for your first job without showing your employer you can communicate well with coworkers or customers.

In the sidebar "The Rewards" on page 4, I mention a few of the benefits of being more social. And I've just illustrated a few more. Social skills are at the core of our daily interactions with everyone in our lives—from family members to the people who sit next to us on the bus. You can try to avoid social situations entirely, but doing so is kind of like trying to avoid getting a pimple. Sometimes, no matter how hard we try to take care of our skin, the pimple still inevitably appears. It's part of adolescence and "growing up." Well, so is being social. Our society is built around it.

According to the *New World Encyclopedia*, the word *society* originates from the Latin *societas*, meaning "a friendly association with others." If you want healthy relationships, meaningful experiences, interesting career options, and the chance to achieve big goals—like traveling to different countries and exploring the world—you have to put yourself out there and learn how to interact with your fellow humans. Learning how to be less awkward when chatting with different people or going to social events is pretty worthwhile.

I hope I've got you mentally nodding along with me. Because I can tell you that developing my own social skills has opened many amazing doors in my life, and now I want the same for you. You can open up new opportunities, build new friendships, and create new memories by learning how to better connect and communicate with people.

No, it's not easy. Yes, it takes practice. Yes, sometimes you may still feel awkward. But when you stop hiding behind your fears and start trusting that you can become more confident in social situations and be someone who feels at ease around others, you'll be amazed at what you'll have the courage to try and experience.

The Who

All kinds of people can struggle with poor social skills. Remember, it doesn't mean you're flawed in any way. It simply means you have to put more effort into communicating with others. But just like you wouldn't shame your friend who had to practice to hit a home run in baseball, there's no reason to shame yourself for needing more practice in social skills.

As we take a look at the different types of people who often suffer from poor social skills, see if there's one that resonates with you the most.

The Introvert

If you consider yourself socially awkward, you may have been referred to as introverted at least once in your life. This has nothing to do with your confidence level; it means you prefer to recharge your energy on your own, while extroverts get energy from being around other people. If you feel drained after being at a friend's party or a school concert, it doesn't mean you're weird. It means the chemical makeup of your brain doesn't need as much external stimulation. You need time to recharge in quieter environments. I'm the same way, which may surprise you. My job involves speaking in front of thousands of people, but at the end of the day, I feel drained and need to be on my own to refresh my energy.

People may interpret your need to be alone as antisocial, but it's okay to step back from the crowd sometimes and take care of yourself. At the same time, it's important you don't let your need to be alone become a habit and an excuse to hide. It's possible to find a happy balance.

The Shy One

If you feel nervous or timid around people, especially ones you don't know well, you may identify yourself as "the shy one." And you're not alone. In fact, psychologists from Stony Brook University found that 20 percent of Americans are born with a personality trait called sensory perception sensitivity (SPS), which can cause people to be more withdrawn around others.

Whether or not SPS is the cause, those who are shy often take time to warm up to others, prefer one-word answers, and would rather "blend into the background" than be singled out in front of a group. There's nothing wrong with any of those things; it just means you have a harder time connecting with people in a meaningful way.

Your shyness may be perceived by others as you being uninterested or uncaring, which I'm sure is rarely the case. It's understandable why they may think that, but we're going to work on building up your skills to help you be more social while also being kind to yourself and understanding that it's okay to feel nervous.

Social Anxiety Disorder

If you feel intense fear when you are around other people and have what feels like a panic attack (for example, a racing heart, shortness of breath, and a tingling sensation in your hands), you may have social anxiety disorder (SAD), also known as social phobia. SAD affects nearly 5 percent of teens. It often stems from an extreme fear of being judged negatively or rejected by others.

SAD can disrupt all areas of your life and be crippling to your social life. You may be so terrified of your friend noticing your trembling hands as you try to pay for lunch or scared you'll have a panic attack during an interview for a summer job that you just avoid those social situations entirely.

If this is a disorder you think you may have, be sure to speak to your parents or a trusted adult about seeking professional help for a diagnosis. I also want you to know that you are not completely helpless in taking back some control over how severely this disorder impacts you and your life. The following chapters will show you how.

Autism Spectrum Disorder (ASD)

In life, some of us have bigger mountains to climb than others. Some people think it's because they're unlucky. I believe it's because their legs are the ones strong enough to hike the steeper climb.

According to the American Psychiatric Association, autism spectrum disorder (ASD) is "a complex developmental condition that involves persistent challenges in social interaction, speech and nonverbal communication, and restricted/repetitive behaviors."

Holding eye contact can be difficult for people with ASD, and they tend to struggle to maintain friendships due to their inability to understand and interpret other people's social cues, such as facial expressions. In extreme cases, ASD can mean the person is nonverbal and unable to communicate in spoken conversations. If you believe you have ASD, please speak to your parents or a trusted adult about seeking medical help for a diagnosis.

If you do have ASD, I want you to know that although your climb may be the steepest of all when it comes to improving your social skills, the strategies in this book will help make it a little easier.

The When

The exciting thing about cultivating your social skills is that it can improve every area of your life. From school and social media to friendships and family life, becoming more confident and competent at connecting with others will make a huge difference. Not only will it strengthen your relationships, but it will also open you up to new opportunities that won't be possible if you keep hiding in the background or not speaking up when it counts.

Let's take a deeper look at how strengthening your social skills will give your life a big boost in the key areas outlined next.

Love

Love: Is there really any better feeling? From the warmth in your heart to the tingle in your toes, love is created in those moments when we feel a deep and intense connection with someone else. It's what bonds families together and inspires two people to come together and create a family of their own. You may be young, but I bet you've felt the warm and fuzzy feeling for someone. Perhaps another person in your grade or someone on your sports team or in your club? Developing these social skills will not only help you find the courage to go and speak to your crush but also actually know what to say, engage with them, and show them you care.

Friendship

Life is better with friends. Whether you're laughing your way through filming a ridiculous TikTok or you're crying on the floor of your bedroom about your parents' divorce, life was meant to be lived with friends by your side. They make the sad moments easier to bear and the happier moments richer. They are people to laugh with, cry with, dance with, play with, explore with, grow with, and learn from. However, just like a flower doesn't grow without the right nourishment, the same goes with friendships. They require time and effort to blossom and thrive throughout the years. Our friends need to feel cared for, understood, and connected to us, which again takes a variety of social skills. But I'm sure you've discovered, as I have, that good friends totally make it worth the effort.

Family

Whether you're an only child or the youngest of five and whether your parents are married or you spend holidays between two sets of parents, the most rewarding—and sometimes most challenging—relationships are the ones we have with our families. You may be super close with your siblings but constantly fight with your mom. Or you may be a daddy's girl but have a brother who's always getting on your nerves. One thing I know for sure is no family is perfect, whatever it looks like. We all have our struggles and conflicts, but family relationships are always worth investing in; they can be a source of unconditional love and support.

I lost my big sister when I was 20 years old, and I can't help but wish I'd taken time to be a little more patient and understanding when she was trying to talk to me. I wish I'd listened more. I wish I wasn't so quick to judge. I can't turn back time, but I can move forward and help you practice these social skills to make your own family relationships even stronger.

School

Quick, name a teacher you can't stand. I know at least one teacher came to mind! The one I struggled with the most in high school was Miss Marsh. She meant well, but she couldn't control the class. It made me dislike science and my grades fell. I decided not to choose any sort of science in my senior year. Looking back, I wish I had, as biology fascinates me now. But back then I didn't have the social skills of active listening, empathy, or confidence to speak up and ask for help with the subject when I needed it.

These are just a few of the skills I'll teach you to help improve your relationships with your teachers and peers so that you don't let them be the reason you don't succeed academically. There's also a ton of great activities—from running for student council to being part of the soccer team or school musical—that require you to have strong social skills to really shine in that arena, so buckle up!

Social Media

I'm going to guess your phone is within arm's reach of you right now. Yes, mine too! It's no surprise since the majority of our socializing these days is done on social media. And I bet your parents are constantly nagging you to spend less time on it. That's not what I'm here to do. I'm here to teach you how to make the most of your communication online so it's done in a way that fosters friendships even when you're not in person. Whether it's a DM on Instagram or a Zoom party with your friends, there are many benefits to communicating with others online. There are also a few things to be mindful of to ensure your online communication doesn't begin to take away from your social skills and ability to connect with others in person.

The Where

Where do you go from here? Have you ever met someone who's superconfident but doesn't seem to care about your opinions? Or perhaps they're a good listener but aren't really great at conversation? Some people tend to be quite good at one or two social skills, but not so much in other areas. This book is meant to help you become an "all-arounder." That means you will discover a complete set of social skills that will help you "read" the room and connect with others. Up next are the five most important social skills we'll be diving into in the upcoming chapters.

Confidence

It may seem strange to think of confidence as a skill, but it actually is. Contrary to popular belief, it's not something you're born with or without. With practice, you *can* become more confident, no matter how insecure you feel right now. Confidence means being able to say to yourself, "I believe in my own value, what I say matters, and I am worthy of being seen and appreciated."

Can you see how believing in yourself could make it easier to strike up a conversation with your peers or speak up when you feel hurt and need to express your point of view? With improved confidence, every area of your social life becomes better. And the good news is that there are a variety of simple strategies you can practice daily to build your self-esteem. We'll go over those in chapter 3.

Emotional Awareness

Imagine you're at school, looking and feeling sad after attending your grandmother's funeral the day before, and your friend comes up and cracks an insensitive joke about grandparents. We would all agree that person lacks emotional awareness.

Emotional awareness is your capacity to recognize and understand your emotions as well as other people's emotions. You probably haven't heard as much about emotional awareness as you have about confidence. But, trust me, it's every bit as valuable, especially when it comes to improving your social skills!

Emotional awareness is especially important when we experience strong emotions like anger or stress. It's very easy to react and lash out when we feel that way. However, having emotional awareness helps us recognize, understand, and manage those feelings in more positive ways so we diffuse stress and conflict rather than add to it. No one teaches us these skills at school, which is why emotional awareness is the topic of chapter 4.

Nonverbal Cues

You know how you can just tell someone is mad by the way their shoulders are hunched over or that they're super excited by their big smile and the sparkle in their eyes? You're picking up on nonverbal cues in those instances. This is often referred to as body language and includes all the different ways we communicate with our bodies, as well as with our facial expressions and eye contact.

Most of these nonverbal cues happen subconsciously, meaning we're not deliberately thinking about doing them; they're often an automatic response to what we're thinking and feeling in that moment. However, it's easy to fall into a habit of displaying nonverbal cues that don't appropriately communicate how we feel or to misinterpret someone else's body language. For instance, that friend with the hunched shoulders? She's not angry; she's actually sad and could really use a friend. Chapter 5 explores how to get better at noticing and understanding other people's nonverbal cues and how to improve your own cues so people better understand you as well.

Active Listening

Have you ever been in the middle of pouring your heart out to a friend about that person who broke their promise and blabbed about your crush on the new guy, and you look up, realizing she's been playing on her phone for the last five minutes? Well, that's exactly what active listening *isn't*. If you've been on the receiving end of a similar scenario, you understand it doesn't feel great to feel not heard by someone.

Instead of being that person, you'll want to work toward becoming an active listener, which means fully concentrating when someone is talking to you and showing subtle signs of engagement. This is how people feel heard and valued. For example, if your friend had been nodding as you poured out your broken heart and saying things like, "It sounds like you are saying you feel betrayed by your friend," you would know she was actively listening to you. And I guarantee you would have felt more connected if she had done this. That's the power of active listening. This is a skill you can improve by practicing the strategies in chapter 6.

Empathy

In the weeks after my sister passed away, I spent a lot of time sitting on my balcony, looking out over the water and crying many tears. I wasn't alone in this pain, though. My beautiful friend Lyndsay would sit there with me. Sometimes she'd put her arm around me and let me cry it all out. Other times she'd reflect back my sadness on her face and say, "I understand you're really hurting right now." In these moments, she was beautifully displaying what's called empathy.

Empathy is the ability to sense and understand how someone else might be feeling and thinking. If you've ever heard someone say, "Put yourself in their shoes," that's what empathy is. It's about imagining how you might feel in someone else's situation, even if you haven't gone through the exact same experience. Even though Lyndsay hadn't lost her sister, she was able to imagine how painful it must be and was able to feel "with me" in those moments. Empathy is a powerful way to build connection in all relationships and is a skill we'll focus on in chapter 7.

The MORE YOU KNOW

I know social media gets a bad rap, but used mindfully—that is, with care and attention—it can be a powerful tool for creating new friendships and connecting with friends, near and far.

According to a 2015 report by the Pew Research Center, more than half of all teens ages 13 to 17 have met a new friend online. Is this true for you, too? I know it is for me. In fact, one of my best friendships started with a Facebook message. The Pew Research Center also found that more than half of all teens say they hang out with their friends online nearly daily, but less than a quarter spend that much in-person time with their friends outside of school and co-curricular activities. Can you imagine a day without sending your bestie a TikTok or watching your friend's Instagram story to see what he's been up to that day? Neither can many other teens!

We know life happens in-person *and* on social media. So we'll also explore how you can tweak some of the tools and strategies to ensure that you're building your social skills for the online world as much as IRL.

TAKEAWAYS

So there you have it! We've just walked through the road map of building your social skills across key areas of your life. We've covered a lot of ground, but here are the important takeaways:

- *Being socially awkward isn't a fixed trait about you. It's something you can change by practicing the strategies you'll learn in this book.*

- *Some people naturally struggle more with social situations, including those who are introverted, shy, suffering from social anxiety disorder, or have autism spectrum disorder.*

- *The skills we're going to focus on to improve your social abilities are:*

  - *Confidence*
  - *Emotional awareness*
  - *Nonverbal cues*
  - *Active listening*
  - *Empathy*

Chapter Two

WHAT YOU BRING TO THE TABLE

This chapter is all about the person holding this book right now—you! We're going to explore why your self-esteem may be low and how to improve it with a few simple strategies to empower your unique strengths and value as a person. We'll also look at why you're never stuck being "just the way you are" and how to process those big emotions when you're in uncomfortable social situations. Best of all, you're going to figure out your short- and long-term goals, which will motivate you as you read the rest of this book. Let's dive in!

SOCIAL SKILLS AND SELF-ESTEEM

"No one really likes me."

That's the answer my teen coaching client gave me when I asked her why she feels awkward at school. She went on to tell me that she sometimes feels invisible to her friends. Have you ever felt that way? As if you're not good enough for people to pay attention to?

This is something many of us struggle with as we enter our teen years because, suddenly, we're not little kids anymore. We are becoming more aware that other people may be judging us, so we're more self-conscious about everything—from the clothes we wear to the TV shows we watch.

You know you're no longer interested in watching *Dora the Explorer*, but what do you want to watch instead? How do you want to style your hair? What sports do you want to play?

These are all totally normal questions to explore throughout adolescence as you try to figure out who you want to be in the world. Unfortunately, we often get so caught up with looking to our peers and social media for the answers that we end up comparing ourselves to how amazing other people are rather than noticing how amazing we are.

Here's a scenario you might relate to: You aren't naturally smart at math like your best friend, and suddenly you're feeling like you're the dumbest person in the grade. Then you see how another friend gets so many likes on her photo, and you start ruminating over how unpopular you are. Then you get home to find out your big brother got a scholarship to college, and you're thinking you're never going to be as good as he is.

All of this "compare and despair" is natural to do because our brains are wired from an evolutionary standpoint to want to be accepted by "the squad." In fact, the same anxiety-inducing fight-or-flight response can be triggered when we walk into a room of strangers where it can feel like we're walking into a circle of tigers. It's very natural for human beings to not like being judged by others, and you're at an age where you're becoming aware of just how often this happens.

Struggling with social awkwardness is a natural part of growing up for many of us. I coach teens on how to overcome it every day, and I'm going to teach you exactly what I teach them: Your thoughts about yourself affect your self-esteem, and your self-esteem affects your social skills and relationships. For example, let's go back to my client who thinks no one likes her (she says it as if she's just stating a fact). She had a lot of evidence for it, too, like when her friends excitedly chatted about what they were going to do on summer break but didn't ask her what she was doing, and it left her feeling upset.

I helped her understand that it wasn't her friends talking about their summer plans that hurt her feelings; it was her interpretation of their actions and thinking, *They don't like me because they're not asking me about my summer plans.* It was her own thoughts and reading of the neutral circumstance that caused her to feel insecure. Once she felt insecure, she was most likely unconsciously removing herself from the conversation by not listening properly or wanting to be seen. As a result, she left herself out of the conversation, which led to a diminished connection with her friends and thus more evidence that "They don't like me."

The way we feel about ourselves drives how we behave and show up in any situation. Those emotions, which come from our thoughts, ultimately drive our experiences in life. Do you catch what I'm saying here? All of your social awkwardness isn't caused directly by the situation you're in—for example, how many people you know at a party. Your social awkwardness is caused by the thoughts triggered in your mind, which then lead to feeling anxious and acting awkward.

The good news is that you can learn how to redirect your mind toward thoughts that can help you feel more confident. When you learn to focus on what you have to offer and what is uniquely wonderful about you, you'll be coming from a place of self-worth, and that will completely change how you show up in any social situation.

As I spoke to my client about this concept, she realized how she could have changed her thinking that day. Instead of thinking, *They're not including me in their conversation about summer plans because they don't like me,* she could have thought, *They're not paying attention to me because they're just so excited about their summer plans. Let me join in the fun by telling them about mine!*

This shift in perspective would have altered her thinking and her mood, encouraged her to feel and act more confident, and ultimately helped her create a stronger connection with her friends.

Embrace Yourself

One of my all-time favorite sayings is: You are 100 percent loveable, and there's nothing you can do about it!

And guess what? It's 100 percent true. Your worth as a human being just is—just like the value of a $50 bill never changes; it's inherently valuable. The same goes for your worth. The trouble is we often forget this. In a society that's always posting the highlight reels online, we think we're only worthy if we look a certain way, get certain grades, have lots of followers, get invited to lots of places— the list goes on, right?! But those are all just external measures that society has made up.

We don't look at babies when they are born and think, *Well, we will love you once you join the football team and have 1,000 followers on Instagram.* No. We love them simply as they are without requiring external measures of worth. And that truth never changes.

Our brains have a built-in negativity bias. This is our brains' tendency to pay more attention to unpleasant stimuli and dwell on negative events, which has been hardwired into us from our cave-dwelling days to help keep us safe. It's also why we are very good at criticizing ourselves compared to others. Here's an exercise to help your brain get better at noticing what is awesome about you and all the different ways you add value to the world, simply by being who you are:

Grab a notebook (or pull up a doc on your computer) and write out as many positive attributes about yourself as you can think of in relation to every single aspect of your life. The list can include 5 things or 50! Here are some examples to get you started:

At Home: I am awesome at helping my mom/dad clean up after dinner.

At School: I am good at getting my homework done on time.

Sports/Extracurricular: I always give my best at piano lessons.

Family Dynamic: I make an effort to be sure my little brother feels included.

Personality: I love to make others laugh.

Siblings: I enjoy helping my sister with her social studies homework.

Work: I am a great after-school tutor.

Self-Empowerment

It's easy to feel like the world is against you some days—your bus is late to school, you get the lowest grade in English, and you hear someone gossiping behind your back, and then you get home to find out that someone you like is dating someone else. Yep, the human brain is very good at noticing these sucker punches because its negativity bias does a really good job of focusing only on the "bad things." It's not so great at noticing our gains or the things we can control to create more wins in our day. Luckily, we can train it to do so! Here's a 30-day challenge I want you to join me in:

My Win for the Day

1. Get a piece of paper and at the top write, "My win for today is . . ."

2. Beneath it, number each line 1 through 30.

3. Each day, write one thing you did, for yourself or someone else, that you consider a win.

For example, maybe you finished your science project or helped your dad clean out the basement. It can be absolutely anything you took action on. There's only one rule: You can't write, "I don't know" or "Nothing" for the next 30 days. There's always *something* you can count as a win, even if it's putting on matching socks or feeding your dog. I know, without a doubt, you've taken control of something today that is worth a pat on the back.

Put this list somewhere you will see every day—on your mirror or at your desk. As you see this "wins list" grow, you'll realize you are far more capable than you know. You might not be able to win everything in your day, but you can always create a win at something. Helping your brain pay more attention to the wins will help you feel more confident. This will inspire you to take action on more wins, which will help you feel even more in control. You will be gaining momentum in the right direction!

A Growth Mindset

If I ask you to water a lamppost every day, you'd likely think I've lost my mind, right? Why on earth would you want to water something that's fixed in concrete and will never grow or change no matter how much effort you put into it?! You wouldn't. That's the definition of *insanity* and a complete waste of time (and water!).

But what if I ask you to water my new plant while I'm on vacation for three months? You would probably be more willing because you know the water will help the plant grow and thrive. You may not see the difference overnight, but with time, you'll see the plant begin to thrive, so it's worth the effort to water it.

Why am I talking about plants and posts? You may still be thinking it's a waste of time to be reading this book because you "just are" socially awkward and there's nothing you can do to change that. But I want you to know that you are not the post—you are the plant.

None of your abilities are fixed. They grow and evolve as a direct result of the amount of effort you put into practicing them. This is because of our brains' neuroplasticity, which is a fancy way to say that our brains, like plastic, are malleable and can be changed with consistent effort. The key is to transition from a fixed mindset ("There's nothing I can do to change the way I am") into a growth mindset ("With deliberate practice and repetition, I can develop my skills, habits, and abilities"). Like watering a plant, the effort you put into something does help you grow and thrive throughout your life.

GET UNCOMFORTABLE

Do you like turbulence on a plane? I hate it. I'm usually a sweaty mess—nails digging into the armrest as my brain starts telling me, "Well, you've lived a good life."

On a recent flight I felt much calmer. Thankfully, the pilot had given us a heads-up before we took off to expect turbulence toward landing. When the turbulence hit, I said to myself, "Oh, hey there, turbulence. I was expecting you. You scare me a little, but ultimately, I know I'm okay."

So that's why I'm giving you the same heads-up: Trying new things is always going to come with discomfort and some turbulence—especially since our brains like familiarity and will sometimes freak out and trigger anxiety when facing something unknown. I suggest you plan on those uncomfortable feelings as you begin to practice the new tips and strategies you'll learn in the upcoming chapters.

I also want to remind you that pilots fly the plane toward the turbulence because they know the plane can handle it. And so can you. You are built for hard things and are capable of handling far more discomfort than you know. I also promise you it is worth learning how to tolerate discomfort. When facing your fears, riding out the discomfort helps you grow into the best version of yourself. Just know we're going to keep flying toward the turbulence, because there are amazing parts of yourself that you still need to meet.

Get Okay with Uncomfortable

Many of us fear emotions like anxiety or nervousness as if they're going to swallow us whole. But I promise you, that's not true. Emotions are simply chemical vibrations in our bodies caused by our thinking. And although we can't always change our thoughts instantly, we can always reduce the intensity of the feelings they are causing. The following exercise will help you do that by practicing how to open up and process your emotion rather than tensing up and resisting it.

Locate it: Where in your body do you specifically feel the emotion? (For example, "I feel it in my stomach, chest, and hands.")

Describe it: What does this emotion feel like in your body? (For example, "There's a racing feeling in my chest, a twisting feeling in my stomach, a pulsing in my forehead, and shakiness in my hands.")

Color it: If this emotion were a color, what color would it be? Giving it a color can help you neutralize the feeling a bit.

Breathe it: To help process the emotion, practice the 4-4-8 breathing exercise: Breathe in for a count of four, hold for a count of four, and breathe out for a count of eight to ensure you fully exhale to bring down your heart rate. Repeat this four times.

Although some feelings are uncomfortable, they are nothing to be afraid of. Our bodies are designed to process emotions just like they're designed to process food. Practicing this exercise will help you learn how to process difficult emotions whenever those big feelings come on.

SET SOCIAL GOALS

When it comes to building your social skills, it's helpful to set a goal that you can use as motivation. You might be unsure about what this goal could be, so this section will help you get clear on your goals, both in the short and long term. A short-term goal is one that can be achieved any time during the next three months. Anything longer than that is considered a long-term goal.

If I told you, "You can have bulletproof confidence for seven days," what's the first thing you would do with this newfound confidence? It could be something you haven't tried because you're afraid to:

- *Invite a friend over to study with you.*
- *Sit at a table with some of your peers at lunch.*
- *Answer a question in front of the class.*
- *Hand in your first job application.*
- *Upload your first vlog on YouTube.*
- *Ask your crush for their phone number.*

Whatever the answer is, you can focus on that as a short-term goal. Now if I told you, "You can have bulletproof confidence for six months," what would you choose to work toward achieving with that confidence? Here are a few ideas:

- *Audition for the school play.*
- *Try out for a sports team.*
- *Upload 10 vlogs on YouTube.*
- *Nominate yourself for student council.*
- *Land your first part-time job.*

I want you to think of something that feels beyond reach right now, but six months from now, you'd love to be able to look back and say you did it! Do you have that thing in mind? Now I want you to supercharge both of your goals by taking two actions:

1. Put a deadline to it. Without a deadline, goals often stay just wishes. So rather than saying, "I'd like to get a job soon," you put a time limit on your goal and say, "I will land my first part-time job by July."

2. Write your goals down and put them somewhere you will see them daily!

This sounds simple, but research has found that you increase the chances of achieving your goals by 42 percent when you write them down. This is because our brains get easily distracted by everything else happening in our lives. Writing down your goals and looking at them daily reminds your brain that this is what you want it to focus on, which increases your motivation toward achieving your goals.

The MORE YOU KNOW

On average, how many hours each day do you spend looking at a digital screen like your phone or laptop?

For the typical American teenager, the answer to that is more than seven hours, according to research by Common Sense Media (and no, that's not counting the time we spend using these devices for homework!). Since we typically sleep for eight hours per day, that means we're spending nearly half our waking hours looking at a digital screen. How do you feel about that statistic?

It makes me want to be more mindful of what I'm missing out on as a result of spending so much time on my phone. Is there homework you're falling behind on or are there in-person conversations you're not paying attention to because you're distracted by your phone? It's just food for thought, as I bet the most meaningful moments of your life haven't come through a screen.

⚡ ⚡ ⚡

TAKEAWAYS

Here's what we've explored in this chapter that you can take forward on the rest of your journey through this book:

- *Social awkwardness is a natural part of growing up for many teenagers.*

- *By focusing more on your positive attributes and "wins for the day," you can increase your self-esteem.*

- *You are not the post; you are the plant. You can grow and evolve your abilities with practice.*

- *If practicing social skills brings up uncomfortable emotions, you can use the strategies in this chapter to process those feelings.*

- *Choosing a short- and long-term goal can motivate you to keep practicing your social skills.*

Next up, we're going to dive deeper into self-confidence: what it is, how we can get more of it, and why it's an important part of feeling more comfortable in social situations.

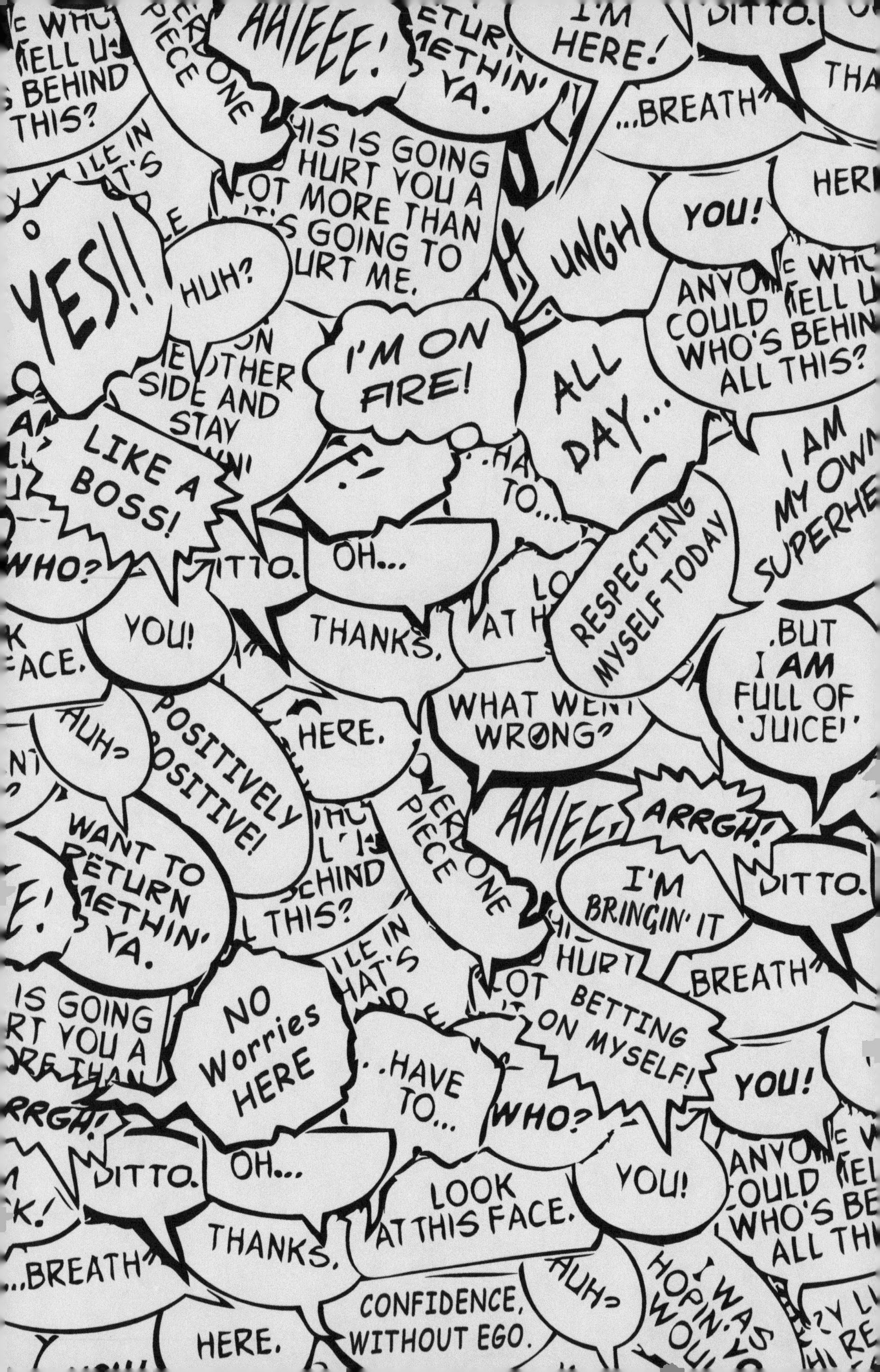

Chapter Three

CONFIDENCE CHECK

Confidence: What does it really mean and how can you get more of it? In this chapter, we'll explore ideas and strategies to help you worry less about what people think of you and care more about standing up for yourself when feeling peer pressure. No matter how insecure you feel now, practicing what you learn in this chapter will boost your confidence big-time.

Confidence Check Scenario

It's the part of the day Jenna dreads the most—lunchtime. Her tray is filled with mac and cheese and she's not quite sure which way to turn.

To the left are the tables where the popular kids sit. To the right are the brainiacs, who she can overhear discussing the midterm exams. In front of her are the jocks who are laughing between massive spoonfuls of food. Whichever way she turns, she feels like she has nowhere to sit. Jenna's been at this high school for a semester, but no one feels like a friend to her.

It's because they think I'm weird, she thinks with a sigh, and her lunch tray begins to feel heavier. No one has saved a seat in class for her let alone asked her to sit with their group at lunch.

What's wrong with me? Why can't I ever make friends? she wonders.

Okay, now she knows it's been long enough, and she can't stand there forever: Time to choose where to sit. Left or right.

I'm too dumb for the smart kids, not pretty enough for the popular girls, she decides.

Her hands begin to shake, and the walls feel like they're caving in. Time is running out, and she swears she can now hear a girl on her right giggling as she whispers into her friend's ear.

Oh no. Now they're all laughing at me and realizing what a loser I am, Jenna thinks.

Her feet feel heavy as she walks slowly toward the left side of the room. She can see there's a spare seat at a table of four other girls whose faces look familiar. She knows one is named Allie because she sat behind her in science the other day and remembers her talking about her new puppy. Oh, how she'd love to hear more about that puppy.

Jenna moves closer to the table, but none of the girls looks up. Her heart is beating out of her chest. She wants to speak up. She wants to say, "Hey, would you mind if I join you?" She so desperately wants to be laughing along with them and to feel a part of the group. Instead, she keeps her eyes to the ground and walks by the girls to the empty table at the back of the cafeteria, like she always does.

WHAT IS CONFIDENCE?

This is one of my favorite ways I've heard confidence described: Instead of thinking, *They will like me,* you think, *I'll be fine if they don't like me.*

And you will be fine because confidence is about believing in your own value. With confidence, your value is never in question nor dependent on someone else's opinion of you. Confidence also helps you show up as who you really are because you embrace all of you—even the parts that don't quite match society's definition of "beautiful" or "cool." You know you have amazing qualities, and you also know you have weaknesses or flaws just like everyone else. That doesn't make you less-than—it makes you human, and above all else, it makes you unique.

Confidence is *not* arrogance. Here's the difference:

- *Arrogance is "I'm amazing and you're not."*

- *Confidence is "I'm amazing and you're amazing. I'm going to appreciate the amazingness in both of us!"*

Confidence means believing the inherent value of not just yourself but also everyone around you. This kind of self-confidence is the foundation for building successful relationships and social skills. It stops you from stressing about what someone might be thinking about you and allows you to relax more naturally into conversations. Rather than hiding in the corner hoping no one notices you at a party, you find the courage to introduce yourself to the guy near you. Instead of awkward silences in the middle of conversations, you're able to notice how pretty someone's necklace is and give them a genuine compliment to make them smile.

Self-confidence is a game changer when it comes to social skills, and the following ideas and strategies will help you create more of it.

None of My Business

Think about how much time you spend each day stressing about what other people think of you, even people who *do not* even matter, like that person you hardly know who follows you online:

- *Will they like my outfit?*

- *Did I say that right?*

- *What will people think if I try that and fail?*

We tend to worry so much about other people's opinions because we think it says something about us. But guess what? It doesn't. Here's why:

Imagine you walk into a party of 20 people you don't know. You hang out for a few hours—they all hear you talk and act the same way. Later, if I asked each person what they thought of you, do you think I'd get the exact same opinion from everyone? Not a chance. I'll get a variety of opinions. And that's because other people's opinions are about them (not you!). For example, you might be wearing a T-shirt that one of them owns so that person thinks you're awesome. You might remind another of a friend's friend who drives them crazy! One person might distrust all people with your color hair after their ex cheated on them with someone who had hair like yours.

Notice what this tells you: Other people's opinions are about them—their past experiences, insecurities, beliefs, preferences, and upbringing—all of which are beyond your control! When you understand that you don't have to take their opinions personally, you release the need to try to control what others think about you. This gives you the freedom to remain focused on yourself and how you want to show up in the world.

Peaches and Preferences

We tend to get into the habit of making other people's opinions mean something about our "enoughness." For example:

They gave me that weird look when I was speaking in class because I'm not good enough.

The reason more people liked my friend's photo over my photo on Instagram is because I'm not pretty enough.

The reason I wasn't chosen for the group assignment is because I'm not smart enough.

We get into the habit of attaching our enoughness, or our sense of self, to how others perceive us. It's no wonder we anxiously try to twist and turn ourselves into the person we think others want us to be. If we were to become that "perfect" person, everyone would approve of us and we could feel better about ourselves. But as we just explored, other people's opinions have nothing to do with us. They're simply telling us about *their* values, preferences, and beliefs.

Here is a powerful mantra to repeat to yourself:

"I can be the juiciest, ripest peach in the world and there's always going to be someone who doesn't like peaches."

And that's totally okay! It says nothing negative about the peach or the person who doesn't like the peach. They're allowed to prefer strawberries. You're allowed to keep being a beautiful peach. The world would be boring if we ALL only loved peaches!

Elephant in the Room

If you are judging yourself right now because you tend to worry about other people's opinions, stop. It's natural for humans to want to feel accepted. We have an innate instinct for connection and a sense of belonging. This also means that every room you walk into, you have something already in common with everyone in it: You all just want to feel like you belong. A powerful way to build that genuine connection with someone is to simply state the elephant in the room, and by that I mean, rather than try to hide your nerves, say, "I'm nervous because I don't know anyone here and feel like a loner."

I've tried this at many parties, and it works every time. There's not a human on this planet who doesn't know how it feels to feel awkward and like an outsider sometimes. Rather than trying to pretend you're not nervous, it's powerful to share it with someone else because people feel connected to vulnerability. Letting your walls down encourages them to do the same. Often the other person will respond with:

- *"Oh, don't worry, I've felt the same."*

- *"Oh, really? Let me introduce you to some people."*

We tend to think that if we share how nervous we are people will judge or laugh at us. More often than not, you'll find they'll relate to you even more. Because humans relate to humans. And part of our humanity includes wanting to feel like we belong. So next time, challenge yourself to be brave and find someone to walk over to and talk with about the elephant in the room.

Reverse the Spotlight

Whether we're about to go to a party or hang out at the mall with a new group of friends, most of us have two thoughts racing through our minds:

- *What are they going to think of me?*

- *Will they like me?*

The focus is always on us. We put ourselves in the spotlight and let our ego get in the way of making genuine connections with people. It's hard to stay present in conversation if your mind is racing with, *Do they like me?* or *Am I interesting enough?*

That anxiety causes our minds to go blank because we're not really paying attention to what's being said. As a result, we fumble our way through small talk and create more evidence that we're "socially awkward." The strategy to overcome this is to "reverse the spotlight." Take the focus off, *Will they like me?* and focus on, *What can I like about them?*

We can't control if someone likes us, but we can control if we like them. Focus on finding what you can like about them. By showing up from a place of "I'm genuinely interested to learn something cool about you," you bring a warm and inviting energy that people can't help but love to be around. When you stop putting yourself in the spotlight, your anxiety reduces and your curiosity increases, inspiring you to open up to the conversation.

Next time you meet someone new, put them in the spotlight by making it your mission to find out one interesting thing about them. Maybe they love art, volunteer at an animal shelter, or speak multiple languages. Whatever it is, there's always something you can find to appreciate about someone. And you know who people like the most? People who like them!

The Rule of Three

If we had a choice, many of us would probably choose to live in a world where everyone loves and supports us. Unfortunately, that's not the reality in this world, and the more we try to make life that way, the more we struggle. We live in a world filled with different values and preferences. Rather than freak out the second you hear that someone talked about you behind your back or laughed at you, practice the "rule of three." Cut the world into three equal pieces in your mind like this:

1. One-third is filled with people who are your haters, bullies, backstabbers, and those who go out of their way to bring

you down. They can *always* find something negative about you. These are the **Sour Worms**.

2. One-third is filled with people who don't necessarily dislike you but also aren't your closest friends or fans. They're acquaintances and peers who you don't speak to often but who aren't unkind to you either. These are the **Toasters** (kind of like toast, they're bland in their opinion of you).

3. One-third is filled with your closest friends and biggest fans. They're the ones who always cheer you on and see the best in you. These are the **Stars**, because that's what they are to you: People who brighten your days.

Although your world might not be filled entirely with Stars, it's also not entirely filled with Sour Worms or Toasters, either. It's usually an equal mix of all three. So, rather than melting down if someone doesn't like you, you can accept that it's perfectly okay. They're just part of the Sour Worms or Toasters. It's not that you should be rude to them, but it also means you shouldn't spend your time changing who you are to try to win them over.

The powerful thing about the "rule of three" is that it gives you back your energy to find your Stars! Your community. The people who love the *real* you, not the person you're trying to twist and turn yourself into. It's impossible to find your true people if you're not showing up in the world as your true self.

Allow room for the Sour Worms and Toasters in your life, but redirect your attention and energy to building friendships with the Stars. They are always out there; you just have to find them.

Confidence Check
Scenario Redux

Let's try this again.

Jenna's tray is still filled with mac and cheese, and she needs to find a place to sit for lunch. As she scans the cafeteria overflowing with students, her heart begins to beat a little faster.

It's okay, she thinks. *There's a group out there that will be happy to have you sit with them.*

She reminds herself that even if some people in the room are Sour Worms, most people are friendly and some of them could even be her Stars—and there's only one way to find them: She has to be brave and put herself out there.

As her eyes scan the room, she sees a girl she recognizes from math class with four other girls at a table that has a spare seat. She feels the buzz of nerves in her tummy as she walks toward the table.

What if they think you're a loser for having nowhere to sit? What if they make fun of what you're wearing or think your glasses look dorky? This negative mind chatter races through Jenna's head, but she takes a deep breath and reminds herself that what someone thinks of her is none of her business. What's more important is focusing on what is within her control: to feel a little bit less anxious.

Set yourself the goal of finding out one interesting thing about each girl—there's always something, she reminds herself.

Then she remembers that the girl from math class, Allie, had spoken about her new puppy in class the other day. *Perfect,* she thinks. *I can at least ask her about that. And maybe see if her friends have any pets as well.*

Before she knows it, she's at the edge of the table, and all the girls are looking up at her. One looks a little hesitant, but Allie breaks out into a smile and says, "Oh, hi, Jenna—that's your name, right? How are you doing?"

continued →

Jenna's heart feels like it's about to beat out of her chest and her hands are a little shaky, but she reminds herself to just be real and address the elephant in the room. "Yes, that's my name: Jenna. I'm doing okay, thanks, but I don't have anywhere to sit for lunch. I feel awkward asking, but you seem really cool so I'm guessing your friends are, too. Would you mind if I joined you while I eat?"

The girl to Allie's right looks a little sour about it, but Allie instantly welcomes Jenna to sit down. There's a slightly awkward silence for a moment and Jenna feels like a deer in headlights, but then she remembers to reverse the spotlight and ask Allie about her puppy.

Allie excitedly pulls out her phone to show her photos of the puppy, which Jenna enjoys seeing. But she can't help but notice the friend beside Allie still looks unsure of her joining the group.

She hates me already, Jenna thinks. But then she remembers that she doesn't even know her yet and should give her a chance. Plus, it's okay. Not everyone can be her Stars, but everyone does appreciate feeling included.

Jenna turns to the friend and says, "Hey, do you have any pets?"

The girl's scowl softens into a slight smile as she replies, "Wait till I show you a photo of my cat, Henry. Pretty sure he thinks he's a dog!"

And just like that the girls spend the rest of lunchtime swapping funny photos and laughing at silly moments with their pets. As the bell rings, Allie asks for Jenna's number and says she's welcome to sit with them anytime.

A smile creeps across Jenna's face as she throws on her backpack and heads to class, proud of herself for stepping outside her comfort zone to practice her new confidence skills.

Alphatude Scenario

It's the fifth period and over 90 degrees outside, and the last thing Tyler feels like doing is going to Spanish class. He turns to Eric and asks, "Hey, man, wanna go down to the mall and get a milkshake with me instead?"

Eric stops walking down the hallway and looks at Tyler. At first, he thinks Tyler is joking, but by the look on his face, Eric knows he's not. A million thoughts race through Eric's mind. For the first time in a long time, Eric feels like he belonged at school today. Tyler asked him to be his lab partner in science and sat next to him in math. Eric so badly wants to make Tyler happy and skip class with him, but . . .

"Oh, come on, dude, Mr. Gladdin won't even know we're not there. You know how clueless he is."

Eric's palms begin to sweat a little. He's never skipped class before. His mom always told him she'd pull him out of soccer if she found out he'd done so. But if he didn't go, would Tyler get angry and stop hanging out with him? Or worse! Would Tyler tell all the other guys in the grade what a wimp he is?

"Don't be a loser. It's just one class. I thought you were cool, but whatev—"

"Okay," Eric interrupts. He can't believe these words are coming from his own mouth: "Let's do it. Let's get that milkshake and hang at the mall."

Tyler smiles and throws his arm around Eric as he heads them toward the school gates. He checks once over his shoulder before they both jump the fence. They think they're in the clear, but little did they know, the vice principal was coming around the corner just in time to see them walking down the street. Vice Principal Jones sighs and turns in to his office to give their parents a call.

WHAT IS ALPHATUDE?

Have you ever asked your friend which movie they want to watch or where they want to go for lunch, but secretly you know you want to watch the new *Avengers* movie, or you are really craving a burrito? Are you too afraid to speak up because you're worried what they may say about your choices? It's possible you have room to grow in practicing your "alphatude," or in plain language, your assertiveness.

Assertiveness is the skill of knowing how to speak up for yourself or others from a place of respect and understanding. This isn't to be confused with aggression or being mean, where you're dismissing or ignoring others' needs and opinions.

Sometimes we're so afraid of coming across as too aggressive that we become too passive. If you don't speak up about your needs or feelings, people may begin to see you as a pushover and try to pressure you into things you don't really want to do or that don't align with who you really want to be.

The solution to this is strengthening your assertiveness skills to help you express your opinions and feelings, ask for what you need, offer your ideas, respectfully disagree, stand up for your values and beliefs, speak up for other people, and be able to say no without feeling bad about it.

Often, we tend to think if we're assertive, we might lose friends. But, in fact, the opposite is true. We often gain and keep friendships—at least the real ones—when we contribute to finding solutions and solving conflicts and when we understand how to communicate respectfully so everyone feels their needs are being met. Consider each of these:

- *Aggressiveness = "That's a dumb idea, do it my way."*

- *Passiveness = "It's up to you, I don't mind what we do."*

- *Assertiveness = "You are welcome to make your own choice, but this is what I'm going to choose to do."*

It's the sweet spot between aggressiveness and passiveness that combines confidence in your own worthiness with the belief that everyone else is worthy of respect and consideration, too. The following strategies will help you develop your ability to be more assertive.

No More "I Don't Know"

Having the confidence to express your own feelings and opinions is a huge part of assertiveness. You can begin practicing this by no longer saying, "I don't know," the next time a friend asks, "Where do you want to eat?" or a family member asks, "What do you want for your birthday?"

If you feel like you really don't know, ask yourself, "If I wasn't worried about what someone was thinking of me, what would I choose?"

That's the answer you want to practice sharing out loud. It may be tricky at first, but try it just one day a week. Challenge yourself to share your preference on every question you're asked. You may be worried that the other person will judge you, but you can work on overcoming that fear with the other assertiveness strategies.

Ask. Ask Again. Ask Some More.

To become more confident in expressing your wants and needs, practice asking for things daily. It could be really simple things at first:

- *"Can I please borrow your pen?"*
- *"What's the time?"*
- *"Do you know when the homework is due?"*

Starting these small requests can help you get accustomed to asking for help, and show you that people are often happy to assist you without judgment. The more you practice with small asks, the more likely you will be able to ask for help on a more important issue.

Value Your Values

It's hard to stand up for yourself when you don't even know what you stand for. That's why it's powerful to get clear on what your personal values are. That means getting clear about the beliefs, qualities, and actions that are important to you and that you want to live by.

Examples of life values include justice, honesty, bravery, and generosity. Getting clear on your values will help when a situation comes in conflict with those values. If you see a friend bullying someone or you're being peer-pressured into drinking, you will recognize it's time to be assertive and stand against those actions. This will help you remain true to who you want to be in the world. Living true to your values is key to inner peace and happiness in life.

How do you discover what your values are? Google "personal values list." You'll find sites that list hundreds of values that you can read about; pick out the top five values that resonate with you. Write them on a piece of paper with the title "This is what I stand for . . ." and put it up somewhere you will see daily. This list will inspire you to be assertive and act in accordance with those values.

Don't Play Dodgeball

If you struggle to be assertive, you likely ask for help in meek and mild ways like, "Maybe you could . . ." or "I was wondering if possibly you can . . ." This gives someone an easy way to dodge the question.

Instead, practice being clear and direct with statements like, "Please, can you . . . ?" or "Will you please . . . ?" These types of statements sound more confident, and the person better understands the specific action or response you need from them. This also means there's a greater chance the request will be fulfilled.

Boundaries

We can't control other people, no matter how hard we try. You can ask all day long for your friend to stop smoking near you or stop pressuring you to try a cigarette, but still, they may continue to do it anyway.

That's why learning how to set proper boundaries is so powerful. A boundary is an expression of what you will do if they don't stop a particular behavior that's in conflict with your needs and values. It's asserting that "If you continue to X, then I will do Y."

- *"If you continue to smoke, I will walk away."*
- *"If you ask me to drink one more time, I will leave the party."*
- *"If you don't stop picking on Johnny, I will tell a teacher about this."*

Boundaries allow people to keep being who they want to be in the world, but they especially help you live true to who you want to be in the world. So think about where in your life you feel that someone may be violating your personal space and values, and decide on the boundary you need to set with them to improve your ability to be assertive and build your self-respect.

Don't Reject Yourself Ahead of Time

We often don't speak up and assert our opinions or needs because we are afraid other people will reject us or be upset with us. We might think, *What if they stop inviting me out places or don't speak to me anymore?* So rather than saying, "Hey, I don't like it when you say that about me" or "I can't go out tonight because I need to finish my assignment," we end up trying to please them.

People-pleasing is when we place other people's needs and wants above our own. So, yes, we may escape possibly being rejected, but do you know what happens instead? We reject ourselves. When we reject our own needs, opinions, and values, it leaves us feeling empty and defeated anyway.

You may be tempted to go along with the crowd to "keep the peace," but there really is no peace either way. Even if you let your friend have it their way and you don't speak up, you can't ignore that inner voice that's begging you to pay attention to your needs. This internal conflict means no inner peace for you.

Practice setting the rule that you will no longer reject yourself in situations that don't align with your values and needs. Yes, you will be risking rejection, but you'll often find that people actually respond with less negativity than you fear. But if they do reject you, that rejection actually has nothing to do with you and everything to do with them (see "None of My Business" on page 36 for a reminder!). Yes, rejection can be uncomfortable in the short term, but it's far less painful than the long-term effects of constantly rejecting who you want to be in this world.

"No" Isn't Selfish; It's Self-Love

I've always loved the quote, "We teach people how to treat us by what we allow." If we want people to love and respect us, we have to love and respect ourselves first. Applying the tips on building assertiveness will help you do this. But let's address the fear that saying no makes you selfish.

Saying no is actually the exact opposite of selfishness. Always saying, "Yes, I'll do that," when you really want to say, "No, I don't want to," leads to underlying resentment in relationships, which causes more conflict in the long run. Setting boundaries and saying no creates healthier relationships because it helps other people learn and understand your needs. By looking after yourself first, you're able to show up with more happiness and love for them. It's a win-win! And if someone does reject you for setting boundaries, they're part of the Sour Worms group, not your Stars (see page 39).

The next time someone asks you to do their assignment for them or to try some alcohol or something else you don't want to do, try saying, "No." That's a complete sentence that protects your best interests, builds self-love, and leads to better relationships.

Let's try this again.

Tyler turns to Eric and asks, "Hey, man, wanna go down to the mall and get a milkshake with me instead of going to Spanish class?"

Eric stops walking and looks at Tyler. At first, he thinks he's joking, but by the look on Tyler's face, Eric knows he's not. He starts thinking how fun it's been to hang out with Tyler in classes all day and how he doesn't want to lose this newfound friendship. But, at the same time, he made a promise to his mom that he'd never skip a class, and he really values how much she trusts in him. He'd hate to destroy that.

"I don't know. Maybe we could . . ." Eric mutters.

"Oh, come on, dude, Mr. Gladdin won't even know we're not there. You know how clueless he is."

Eric's heart begins to race, and he thinks, *He's going to be so mad at me if I don't do this with him. What if he tells all his friends to ignore me from now on?*

The fear of rejection rises in Eric's chest. Then he remembers not to reject himself ahead of time. Eric will be upset at himself if he follows through with Tyler's plan. *Stop playing dodgeball, Eric*, he thinks. *Just say it.*

Eric turns to Tyler, looks him in the eyes, and says, "Tyler, I've had a really fun day with you, but I'm not going to skip class. We have that science exam soon and my mom would kill me if she found out. I can't stop you from going, but sorry, buddy, you're on your own with this one."

"Don't be a wimp. It's just one class. I thought you were cool but whatever."

The sting of humiliation burns in Eric's chest as he sees Tyler stomp off down the hallway. But then Eric takes a deep breath and internally gives himself a high five. He knows that if he'd gone along, he'd be stressed about getting caught and wouldn't be able to handle the look on his mom's face if that happened. Plus, he knew if he did it this one time, Tyler would just keep asking again and again, and he didn't want to get in the habit of skipping school. It wasn't who he wanted to be in the world.

The MORE YOU KNOW

If you've experienced peer pressure, you're not alone. In fact, 86 percent of teens have been peer pressured by their friends, according to a 2018 survey at St. Ursula Academy based in Cincinnati, Ohio. It wouldn't be surprising if that was the national average. And the real problem lies in the fact that most of the behavior you're being pressured into is either risky, illegal, unkind, or discriminatory. You end up taking action to win over people who aren't even really "your people." It's a lose-lose.

The ones who are truly meant to be your Stars will always respect your boundaries. And the only way to discover who they are is to practice being assertive when you need to be—starting now.

TAKEAWAYS

The skill of confidence is like a chocolate layer cake—there are many tiers to it. To put it all together into one delicious bite for you, here are the key takeaways:

- *Confidence isn't arrogance; it's believing in the inherent value of everyone, including yourself.*

- *What other people think of you is none of your business because it's a reflection of who they are not who you are.*

- *Being more assertive takes practice, but it's worth it to live true to your values and to discover your real friends.*

Next, we're going to take a look at emotional intelligence—and no, it doesn't mean how smart our emotions are. It's something so much more!

Chapter Four

BUILD YOUR EQ

Roller coasters are meant for thrill rides, not for our everyday emotions. Yet I know that when I was a teenager that's exactly how my emotions felt—here, there, and everywhere! Perhaps you can relate. One second you're totally chill, and the next second your frustration goes through the roof. The skill that helps you get a handle on this roller coaster is what we'll be exploring in this chapter—emotional intelligence, also known as emotional quotient or EQ.

"Well, Shaun, meet my daughter, Jessica."

With her eyes on the ground, Jessica barely acknowledges what her mom has just said. She doesn't want to be in this restaurant right now, let alone meeting her mom's new boyfriend. She keeps staring down and playing with her bracelets.

Shaun clears his throat, "Well, hello there, Jessica! So good to finally meet you! I've heard so much about you, all good, of course!" Shaun shifts uncomfortably in his chair as Jessica slowly raises her eyes to meet his.

Jessica stares for a moment and feels heat rising in her chest. She's pretty sure if she opens her mouth right now all that will come out is a scream.

Jessica's mom looks desperately between the two, trying to think of something to say. She so badly wants them to get along but knows that Jessica has had a hard time since the divorce two years ago. "Jessica, did you hear, Shaun?" she says finally. "He said hello. It would be nice for you to at least acknowledge him."

Jessica darts her eyes back at her mother with a furious look. "Are you serious, Mom? Well it would have been nice for you to at least think about us kids before you went and left Dad!"

The people at the table next to them turn to stare, but Jessica goes on anyway, "You only ever think about yourself and now you're going to let this guy steal you away from me? Well, guess what? I don't want to meet Shaun and I don't want to be here. So, I'm out!"

Jessica stands up, slams in the chair she was sitting on, and storms out of the restaurant in tears but not before nearly colliding with a waiter holding a tray full of food.

WHAT IS EMOTIONAL AWARENESS?

If you've ever hung out with a toddler for a few hours, you've likely witnessed a tantrum over a simple thing like not getting a lollipop or having to take a nap. That's because they're lacking what this chapter is all about—emotional awareness. This is your ability to recognize and regulate your own feelings.

Although toddlers can be given a pass since they haven't quite yet developed emotional awareness, teenagers should be at a stage in their lives where they can regulate their own feelings. If they haven't yet developed that skill, some teens can act like "grown-up" toddlers—yelling, arguing, crying, and having meltdowns over things they can't control.

The inability to regulate your emotions or control the things you say or do in the heat of the moment may not only feel like you're on a roller coaster, but can also damage important relationships and goals. The solution to getting off the emotional roller coaster is understanding how to notice your feelings, recognize their root cause, and focus on finding healthy ways to process those feelings.

Building your emotional awareness skills will improve every area of your life, including dealing with bad grades, navigating personal relationships, and handling challenging setbacks and conflicts. When you learn how to intentionally respond to your emotions, rather than freaking out with a knee-jerk reaction, you get the power back to decide how you show up in the world, especially in social situations. Let's explore more about emotional awareness in the following sections and then look at some strategies for increasing it.

Self-Management

Once you become a teenager, you really crave a sense of control over your own life. Learning the skill of self-management is a huge part of this. It's like becoming your own boss. You are taking responsibility for your own thoughts, feelings, and actions and better controlling the way they impact you and other people. It's stepping out of the blame game and no longer acting on impulse. It's about taking a moment to pause and respond with deliberate thought instead of heated emotion.

This takes practice because our brains often run on autopilot. But with the right tools, you can learn how to better manage your emotional reaction in even the most difficult situations.

Self-Awareness

One thing many of us feel certain about is how other people should or shouldn't be in the world. "They shouldn't say that" or "They shouldn't be so angry or upset." We are so quick to pay attention to how others react and behave, and we pay less attention to how we feel and react. To build healthier relationships with others, it's important to be aware of how you show up in social situations. And how you show up depends on your thoughts, your feelings, and your actions. That means you have control.

You can start by paying attention to your feelings, which are based on what you're thinking, and then reflect on whether they're helpful thoughts before allowing them to overtake your reaction toward someone else.

Social Awareness

Social awareness is "the ability to understand and respond to the needs of others," according to psychologist Daniel Goleman. For example, if you were talking to a grandparent who is losing their hearing, social awareness means speaking loudly and more slowly than if you were speaking to one of your friends. Or if you're in the quiet section of the library, social awareness means making sure you're not laughing or talking too loudly. This skill is about being mindful of where you are and who you're talking to, and how you can best adapt your behavior to the needs of both. Combining social and emotional awareness means developing the ability to connect and communicate with people in a way that helps them feel respected and valued.

Relationship Management

Have you ever said something in the heat of the moment that in retrospect you're not proud of? Yeah, me too. Relationships can be both fulfilling and challenging. When they're going well and everyone is happy and in agreement, they are wonderful. However, when things aren't quite so peachy and there's a difference in opinions or values—like the friend who is upset you didn't invite her to your sleepover last week or your mom who is nagging you about tidying up your room—relationships can sometimes get tense and tested.

As human beings, we're tempted to get defensive and lash out by complaining or blaming, or we completely shut down and push others away in shame. Either way, neither of these options leads to good outcomes and sometimes can be the end of a relationship. Thankfully, it doesn't have to be that way. There are skills you can learn to better manage relationships, so they don't turn into a wreck every time you don't agree on something. Staying out of the blame game and stepping into a more open-minded place of compromise, patience, and empathy is the key to becoming a better friend, sibling, student, teammate, daughter, or son.

What's *Really* Causing How You Feel?

Emotional awareness is all about being aware of what you're feeling and why you're feeling it. The best way to figure that out is to "brain dump" your mind onto a piece of paper and get curious about what's happening in your internal world. So, grab your journal, and for the next seven days, practice doing a daily "thought download" by answering these questions:

1. What were my three main emotions today? A feeling is a physical sensation in your body that you can describe in one word, such as *anxious, excited, ashamed, motivated, angry, happy,* or *stressed.* Anything longer is a thought.

2. Pick the most uncomfortable emotion, and explain what you think happened to make you feel that way. For example, "My friends ignored me again and didn't care enough to invite me out to lunch with them."

3. Now write down just the basic facts of the situation, without judgment or opinion. For example, "My friends did not invite me to lunch." Notice that when you state just the facts, all situations are neutral. People and events do not cause our feelings; only our own thoughts and interpretations of what happened do.

4. Now look back at what you wrote in question two and finish this sentence: "The real reason I feel this way is because I think . . ."

5. Take a moment to question that thought by asking, "How might I be wrong about this?" Write down one piece of evidence that proves your current thought is false. For example, "My friends do care about me. One of them replied to my text yesterday." If you believed this thought instead, consider how differently you'd feel and act around your friends. This is how you know it's your thinking that influences your emotions, which is the best news because it's the one thing you can always question and change for the better.

Like a Pancake, Flip Your Complaint into a Request

Would you be more likely to get defensive if someone says to you, "I can't stand it when you leave the towels on the floor! You're so messy!" versus "Can you please hang up the towels after your shower? It helps keep things tidy." You chose the first statement, right?

No one really enjoys being criticized or having someone tell them what they're doing wrong. It can cause extra tension and lead to an argument because most of us will argue back when criticized. Instead, it's more effective to turn your complaint into a request that clearly outlines what you prefer. If your request is framed in a positive way, you're likely to receive a positive response that complies with your desires.

The next time you feel the urge to complain about how loud your sister is or how late your friend always is, flip the pancake. Instead of "You're so selfish! You're always running late" try "Can you please message me when you're running late so I know when you'll arrive?" The other person is more likely to cooperate, and you'll get what you want.

Take Off Your "Skepticals"

Our brain's negativity bias (see page 22) is always on the lookout for "bad things" and is quite good at criticizing us and others. It's as if we're always wearing "skepticals" (like spectacles, but with a negative lens). It usually creates unnecessary stress and frustration for us.

The next time you feel that negativity bias overcome you, rather than immediately reacting to it, pause for a moment and ask yourself, "What are the positives my skepticals are blinding me to right now?" When you wear skepticals, you'll always be missing something—so try taking them off.

Don't React, PAC (Pause, Ask, and Challenge)

Whether you're embarrassed because you are stumbling through your speech in front of the class, you're upset because your friends didn't invite you to go out with them, or whatever uncomfortable emotion you're feeling, the PAC strategy is a simple but powerful tool to get a handle on your emotions. PAC keeps your mind from running wild with thoughts, which can keep your emotions from running wild, too. Here's how it works:

Pause: Take a moment to stop and breathe before you react to something. This helps train your brain to pay more attention to your inside world than to your outside one. If there's one skill vital to developing emotional awareness, it's the pause, because it gives you an opportunity to ask this next important question:

Ask: "What am I thinking that makes me feel this way?" This question helps you become aware of your perspective, which will explain your feelings and reaction in the moment. It also helps get your power back and out of "blame mode." The next time you're having trouble speaking up in class, ask yourself what you're thinking that's causing you to feel frustrated. It's not that you're mixing up your words or your hands are trembling; it's because you're thinking, *I'm such an idiot. I can never speak in front of others.*

Challenge: Once you've recognized the thought behind your emotions, challenge it to see that it really is just a story in your mind and not the truth. Ask the million-dollar question: "If someone gave me a million dollars to prove this thought is false, what evidence could I find?" Our brains don't notice certain things until we tell it to step back and view a situation in a different light. For example, sometimes you *do* manage to share your answer in front of the class without freezing up or you are able to talk comfortably in a group if it's about a topic you're really interested in. So, it's not true that you can *never* speak in front of others. When you realize your thought is false, it loses its power over you and your emotions, and you're open to taking on a new and more useful perspective.

Practicing PAC whenever you feel frustrated will help you learn how to calm yourself and manage your emotions in any social situation.

My Best Self

I know it's easy to shout back at your mom when she takes your phone away, or you may be tempted to spread a rumor about your friend after you heard she was gossiping about you behind your back. These actions are driven by fearful and revengeful emotions like frustration, anger, and intolerance. Although it's natural to feel these emotions initially, after your thoughts are automatically triggered, you don't want to act upon these feelings as if you had no choice. You *always* have a choice.

When I'm tempted to blame or lash out at someone, I say, "Okay, brain, I see you're pretty upset right now. But tell me, how would my best self show up in this situation?" This stops my brain from dwelling on vengeful thoughts and allows me to choose how to respond.

We each have a "best self." This is the part of you that believes in everyone's worthiness, including your own. It also knows there's no upside to blame and negativity. Think of your best self as being rooted in love, compassion, and bravery. I always think about a girl who shows up from a place of courage and kindness. Then, I think about how she would respond to someone spreading a rumor about her. Would she allow her anger to make her jump on Snapchat to start the gossip train and try to get the person back? Or would she take a moment to breathe, call a trusted friend to let off some steam, and then decide to just let it go?

My best self will always choose the latter, and I believe yours would, too. You can tap into your best self for guidance at any time in any situation by pausing, taking a breath, and asking for it. Let your best self have a say before you lead with your emotions.

They're Doing the Best They Can

I choose to believe that everyone is just doing the best they can. If your friend gives you the cold shoulder because you forgot to reply to a text or your teacher yells at you for being late, remind yourself that they are doing the best they can at that moment. That doesn't mean their best is great, but it accepts a fact we tend to forget: They are human, too. Your mom is human. Your friend is human. Your teacher is human.

You know what that means? Sometimes they're going to make mistakes, feel insecure or stressed out, and do things that may be unfair. It's not because they hate you. It's because they're human. And so are you.

Give people the same compassion and understanding you wish for yourself when you mess up. We tend to treat others and ourselves so much better when we believe in the goodness of humanity. We sure aren't perfect, but there's always something to love about everyone.

Chill Zone

Meditation is a powerful way to help manage your stress or anxiety and increase your emotional awareness. You don't have to become a yogi to do this. There's no perfect way to meditate, and it's okay if you can't sit still for more than a few minutes.

Taking just five minutes a day to focus on your breathing while listening to peaceful music can have a huge impact on your mental well-being. My favorite meditation app is Insight Timer, which offers more than 55,000 free meditations of different lengths and genres.

Set a goal for the next 30 days to listen daily to a five-minute guided meditation. It will help you practice detaching from your thoughts and releasing the emotional charge they're causing. Meditation has been powerful in my life and helps calm me down. You have nothing to lose and lots of peace of mind to be gained! (I suggest letting your parents know you've set this goal and deciding together on the best time for you to do it based on your commitments.)

Emotional Awareness Scenario Redux

"Well, Shaun, meet my daughter, Jessica."

Jessica is instantly frustrated and wishes the ground would swallow her whole. She really doesn't want to be meeting her mom's new boyfriend. He's just trying to get between her and her mom.

Shaun clears his throat and says, "Well, hello there, Jessica. It's so good to finally meet you! I've heard so much about you, all good, of course!"

Jessica feels heat rising in her chest and is tempted to yell at him to go away and leave them alone. Instead, she takes a deep breath and tells herself, *Pause for a second, Jess. Don't just flick the switch.*

"Jessica, did you hear Shaun? It would be nice for you to at least acknowledge him."

Jessica is irritated. But then she looks at her mom's worried face and feels the frustration release as she thinks, *Mom is just doing the best she can.*

"Oh, sorry. Hi, Shaun," Jessica mumbles politely.

She knows it's not really her mom's fault she's angry. She also knows it's her thoughts that influence her feelings. A moment ago, she was thinking that Shaun was trying to get between her mom and her. So, she asks herself, *If I could get a million bucks to prove this thought is false, what evidence could I find to support that?*

Jessica realizes Shaun made the effort to include her for lunch when it could have been just him and her mom. *That's strong proof he's not trying to get between me and my mom. He's actually making an effort to build a relationship with me, too,* she thinks.

"It's so nice to have you here, Jessica," Shaun says. "Your mom tells me you love sushi. What's your favorite?"

Wow, it's kinda cool he knows a few things about me, Jessica thinks. "It's usually salmon and avocado, but today I'm in the mood for chicken teriyaki," she says with a smile.

continued →

"No way! That's one of my favorites, too!" Shaun smiles back, as he fills up her water glass. "Now tell me, what's the best movie you've seen this year? I need some suggestions."

Jessica smiles because movies are definitely her thing.

By taking a moment to practice PAC rather than just react, Jessica helps the three of them have a nice lunch full of friendly banter. It's clearly the start of a great relationship between Jessica and Shaun.

The MORE YOU KNOW

Are you embarrassed that it takes you ages to make a friend? Well, listen to this: A 2018 study published in the *Journal of Social and Personal Relationships* discovered you have to spend about 50 hours with someone before thinking of them as a casual friend, 90 hours to grow into "real friends," and 200 hours to build a close friendship. Two hundred hours is equivalent to spending every hour of every school day with someone for five straight weeks. And, of course, at school, you don't spend every single minute with your peers.

So the key thing to remember here is that friendships take time, so if you've started to make an effort to interact more with others, keep making that effort—you're right on track!

TAKEAWAYS

Well, you've learned a lot about emotional intelligence and self-awareness in this meaty chapter. Here are a few key takeaways:

- *Emotional awareness is the ability to recognize and regulate your own feelings.*

- *Contrary to popular belief, circumstances and other people don't cause your feelings. Your thoughts are what create how you feel in any given situation. This is good news because changing your thoughts gives you the power to change your emotional reaction for the better.*

- *Unlike IQ, your EQ isn't a fixed trait. You can develop your emotional intelligence using the strategies explored in this chapter.*

Now we're going to dive into a social skill that your ear can't hear but your mind can read: body language.

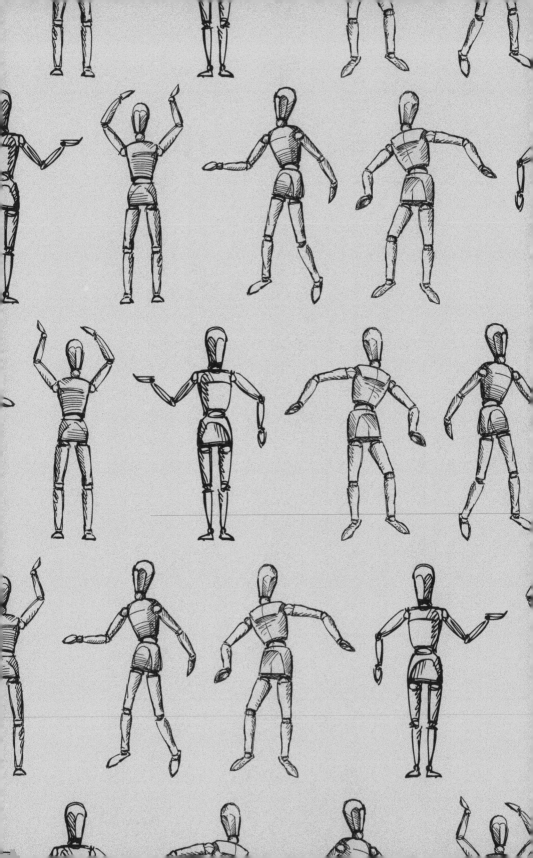

Chapter *Five*

BODY TALK

The most ancient form of all communication is body language. It's how humans communicated before words were ever spoken, and it's still very much a part of how we understand each other today. The problem is sometimes we forget to pay attention to someone's posture or facial expressions and misread what they're saying, or we forget to notice our own body language and inadvertently give off a different vibe than we intended. That's why this chapter is all about building up the social skill of reading and expressing body language to better understand others and help others better understand you.

Body Talk Scenario

"So, Mario, what do you like to do outside of school?"

Hunched over in his seat, Mario is staring at the ground. He's anxious about his first job interview and his heart is pounding in his chest. He wants this job so badly to help pay for his first car.

"Sorry, did you hear me, Mario?"

Wendy has interviewed many teenagers for the job at her family-run restaurant, and Mario seems like a nice kid, but she's not sure he's even interested.

"Uh, yeah, sorry. Um, I like to play video games and skateboard sometimes." His eyes dart up to Wendy's and then back to the ground as his hands dig deeper into his pockets.

"Oh, nice. And why do you love skateboarding so much?" Wendy can't put her finger on it, but something seems a little off-putting about Mario.

He shrugs his shoulders and mumbles something quietly.

"Sorry, Mario, I didn't hear that."

"I said, 'It's fun to do.'"

Wendy thinks she heard slight hostility in Mario's voice as if he was annoyed she'd asked twice. Even though she doesn't like the vibe she's getting, she relaxes into a smile because she knows job interviews can be unnerving.

"Oh, okay, well that's good then. So why do you think you would make a good waiter here?" she asks, hoping Mario will relax a little.

Mario folds his arms across his chest and sighs. It's not that he doesn't want the job; he just wants the interview to be over. He doesn't like talking about himself to anyone. And he has no idea how to answer the question. Hoping to speed up the interview, he pulls his phone out of his pocket.

"Am I keeping you from something?" Wendy asks with irritation. "Let's just end the interview here. I'll call you if you get the job."

Wendy never calls.

WHAT IS BODY TALK?

From an eye roll to the way we cross our legs, our nonverbal social cues convey a lot. It all falls under "communication that occurs without words." In fact, researchers have found about 70 percent of our communication comes from nonverbal cues like posture, facial expressions, eye contact, and tone of voice. I've devoted a whole chapter to it because it's not just what you say but how you say it that matters. It's not just our mouths doing the talking.

As humans, we intuitively pick up on other people's feelings or motives through their body language and nonverbal communication. Like that friend you knew was upset because his shoulders were slumped over, or when you knew your sister had a confession to make because she kept biting her lip and avoiding eye contact before admitting she lost your jeans. Without being aware of it, you are always reading and interpreting other people's body language, and they're doing the same to you. They notice your arms across your chest or that you're fidgeting with your phone when they talk to you. You may think you're hiding how anxious or uninterested you are, but your nonverbal cues are saying otherwise. Your cues can "make or break" the outcome when you are trying to connect with people and build relationships.

In the following sections, we'll look at the main types of nonverbal cues to pay attention to followed by simple tips to build your skills in this area. This is a skill that's going to be increasingly important as you start interviewing for part-time jobs and even college admissions, where first impressions matter. Let's dive in!

Tone of Voice

Have you ever texted a friend and they totally misunderstood what you were saying? Maybe you texted, "It doesn't matter," and they thought you were upset so they got defensive. But you were actually saying it in a lighthearted way to cheer them up. This mix-up likely happened because an essential part of effective communication was missing—tone of voice.

Your tone of voice can convey feelings and intentions like sincerity, sarcasm, humor, anger, excitement, and curiosity. It influences how someone interprets what you're saying and how they feel about your words. For example, if you sarcastically shouted, "Well, aren't you just the best?!" versus softening your voice and playfully saying, "Well, aren't you just the best!" you will get a different reaction in each instance. Your tone conveys intention based on the words you emphasize and the inflection of your voice.

Given all you're conveying in your tone, it's quite important to be mindful of the tone you choose so you're not sending the wrong message.

Facial Expressions

Chances are you've heard your parents say, "Don't give me that face!" Without saying a word, you've already expressed your frustration with them. How? Because your inward slanting eyebrows and pouting mouth say it all. That's the power of facial expressions. They convey your feelings, mood, and attitudes and are one of the most universal languages in the world. No matter where you travel, everyone recognizes a smile as a signal of friendliness or happiness. Your facial expressions are a powerful part of communicating with others, whereas noticing and understanding other people's facial expressions helps them feel respected and listened to, which helps build a connection between you.

Eye Contact

Are you uncomfortable looking someone in the eye when you're talking to them, especially if you don't know them well? You're not alone. Most people who struggle with social awkwardness feel the same. If you have social anxiety disorder (SAD) or are on the autism spectrum, it's even more extreme. Research shows that eye contact, specifically in those with SAD and autism, can trigger your amygdala, the part of the brain that warns of danger, so it's natural if you find eye contact uncomfortable.

However, a lack of eye contact is often interpreted as a lack of interest and can breed mistrust. (Think of how liars tend to struggle to look you in the eye.) Although you may be struggling to maintain eye contact because of your insecurities, the other person may begin to feel disrespected and unworthy of your attention. On the other hand, if you intently stare someone in the eye without looking away, the other person may feel intimidated or threatened. Scientists have found the sweet spot of just the right amount of eye contact is three to four seconds. If this sounds like a long time to manage right now, that's okay. Practicing the skills you learn in this book will help you feel more confident, which will help eye contact come more naturally.

Hand Gestures

Although you want to be careful to not overuse hand gestures, using your hands while you speak can help keep someone's attention, and they will often better remember what you say, research has found. Whether it's to emphasize a point you're trying to make or give instructions, hand gestures are used universally around the world.

However, not all hand movements carry the same meaning! Across cultures, gestures can communicate different things. For example, in the United States, curling the index finger with your palm facing up is commonly used to call someone closer. In many Asian countries, that same gesture is considered very offensive. With that said, many gestures are more common across cultures, including:

- *Having open palms by your side = Sign of friendliness and honesty (This goes back to our ancestors' days where seeing someone's hands meant they didn't have any weapons to harm us.)*

- *Burying your hands in your pockets or tucked across your chest = Sign of suspicion and disconnection (This is definitely something we want to avoid.)*

Posture

If you struggle with low self-esteem, you probably have a tendency to slouch your shoulders and hang your head when you're with a group of people, hoping you can "disappear" into the background. But if you're always trying to hide away, it's much harder for people to connect with and get to know you. Slouched shoulders can actually convey a sign of disinterest.

In the context of going on your first job interview or auditioning for the school play, your hunched-over posture will convey the message that you don't care that much or you lack confidence in your ability. Conversely, pulling your shoulders back with a straight and upright posture and not fidgeting with your phone or your hands conveys confidence and a keen interest in those around you, helping you better connect with others.

Personal Distance

Ever been in line at the counter for lunch and someone stood way too close to you? Yeah, it's definitely not a comfortable feeling. That's why keeping a comfortable distance between you and the person you're talking to is important when it comes to nonverbal social skills. Your relationship with the other person will determine the appropriate amount of space needed. Here's a general rule of thumb:

Intimate Distance: Anything from touching to 18 inches of space. This is usually only for your closest relationships, like hanging on the couch with family, hugging your best friends, or holding hands with your boyfriend or girlfriend.

Personal Distance: From 18 inches to 3 feet apart. This is what you'd typically find comfortable with your peers, teachers, and people you feel familiar with.

Social Distance: From 3 feet to 6 feet apart. This is the distance you would use when just meeting someone for the first time or interacting with people you don't know that well.

This doesn't mean you need to get out a ruler every time you meet someone. It means, remember to be mindful of the distance between you and the other person. Standing too close to someone can be perceived as creepy, whereas standing too far away can give the impression you don't want to be near them at all.

Aim for Three to Four

Always make an effort to establish eye contact with someone at the start of a conversation, and then aim to maintain eye contact with them for about three to four seconds—that's about how long it would take you to register their eye color. And when you stop looking at them, avoid darting your eyes quickly to the ground or all over the place because that communicates a sense of nervousness. Instead, slowly glance away to the side before resuming eye contact with them again a couple of seconds later. Maybe you can practice this with someone you feel comfortable around to help it become more natural, and little by little you will find it easier to do!

You Don't Always Have to See Eye to Eye

If looking into someone's eyes is too much for you right now, a step toward this is to look somewhere near their eyes—like their nose, brows, or space between their eyes. I do this sometimes when I'm feeling nervous about giving a presentation to hundreds of people. I look just above their brows, and it helps calm my nerves.

Ideally, you'd like to get to a place where you can comfortably look into someone's eyes for three to four seconds, but somewhere on their face is a lot better than staring at the ground or in a completely different direction. To get comfortable with this idea, practice looking at your nose in the mirror while you brush your teeth.

It's Not What You Say but How You Say It

This exercise can help you use the appropriate tone of voice to match your emotion, as well as improve your ability to notice someone else's tone of voice to tune in to how they're feeling.

Practice saying the following sentence out loud or to a sibling or parent: "My friend is coming over tomorrow." Say it in an excited voice, then in a surprised voice, and then in an angry voice. Can you hear the difference? By speaking the same sentence in a different tone of voice, you completely change the emotional message behind it. Your excited voice conveys that you are happy while your angry voice conveys the opposite.

This week, pay attention to someone's tone of voice when they are speaking to you so you can respond appropriately to how they're feeling. Also notice if your tone of voice aligns with the emotions you're feeling about what you're saying. If you're excited to see someone, make sure they can hear it in your voice!

Out of Your Pockets and into the Box

Straight up I am going to say, "No more pockets!" If someone is speaking to you or you're speaking to someone (or to a room of people), keep your hands out of your pockets. It makes people feel uneasy and shows a lack of confidence in what you're saying.

Body language experts recommend using your hands when you communicate with others but also that you stay in "the box." That means keeping your hand gestures between your waist and the top of your chest. That space is considered the most appropriate. Bigger hand gestures can be seen as intimidating or distracting.

Practice this in the mirror. Talk about dinner last night or a topic you find interesting, keeping your hands out of your pockets and inside "the box."

Let's Face It

Practicing your social skills doesn't always have to be hard. Just for fun, I recommend getting curious and watching the way people's expressions change throughout a conversation. This may be easiest to do with someone you know well, like your parents or siblings. Pay attention to the changes in their eyebrows and mouth as they chat with you. Facial expressions are important to understanding someone's emotional state. Sometimes you catch looks on someone's face that speak way louder than words.

When you ask someone how they're doing, look at their body language and their facial expressions. Maybe they said, "I'm okay," but their hunched-over posture, crinkled brows, and sad eyes say otherwise. Believe their body language more than their words and respond appropriately to what you sense they are truly feeling.

Straighten Up and Smile

I'm sure you've heard, "Don't slouch!" once or twice in your life. And forgive me for sounding like your mom or dad, but sitting or standing up straight with your shoulders pulled back can make a huge difference when interacting with others.

You don't have to suddenly become as stiff as a board. Focus on not letting your shoulders hunch over, keeping your hands naturally by your side, and don't fidget. Slouching and crossing your arms can be interpreted as a sign of boredom, anxiety, or disinterest—not exactly the vibe you're going for on a job interview or first date. Instead, stand tall, and remember a smile means the same thing in any language. When you smile, the world can't help but smile with you.

Body Talk Scenario Redux

"So, Mario, what do you like to do outside of school?"

Mario realizes he's slouching in his seat, so he straightens himself up and leans in a little as he looks Wendy in the eyes for a moment. "Well, ma'am, I love skateboarding every afternoon and enjoy playing video games with my friends."

"Oh, that's wonderful! My eldest son loves skateboarding, too!" Wendy exclaims. Even though she only met Mario a few minutes ago, she likes how he's carrying himself with keen interest. "How long have you been skateboarding?" she asks, tilting her head with a curious smile.

Mario smiles back and says in a playful voice, "I've been riding skateboards since I was in diapers!"

Wendy laughs and replies, "Well, we can't serve our customers on skateboards, but why do you think you'd make a great addition to our team?"

Mario takes a moment to think and then looks Wendy in the eyes. He leans in a little more and says, "You know what, ma'am? I know I don't have any special skills right now, but I am a fast learner and will do what it takes to become the most valuable employee."

As he speaks, Mario lifts his right hand and extends his index finger to convey the idea of him becoming the "number one" employee to back up his confident answer. He holds Wendy's gaze for three seconds before thoughtfully looking away for a moment, ready for his next question.

"Well, Mario, I do like the sound of that. It's not always about being the best but giving your best! That's all I have to ask for today. I'll give you a call if you get the job."

Mario gets the call three days later.

The MORE YOU KNOW

Most of us don't go anywhere without our phones. They're essentially an extension of our bodies these days. But, as important as our phones are to us, they often serve as a distraction when we're speaking with someone. If you're paying attention to your phone while someone is talking, you could be missing out on reading important cues from their body language.

A 2018 study on digital distraction found that, during a meal, participants who placed their phones facedown on the table felt less enjoyment and connectedness, as well as more boredom and distraction, than those who actually put their phones away. So, at your next meal, put your phone in another room to see if you feel more connected with who you're talking to. I've definitely noticed a difference!

TAKEAWAYS

Let's look at some of the key points we explored in this chapter so you can keep them in mind moving forward:

- *About 65 percent of our communication is through nonverbal cues, which give clues to how you're really feeling or the point you're trying to make.*

- *Nonverbal cues include everything from eye contact and tone of voice to posture and personal distance.*

- *Although body language happens naturally based on how you're feeling, you can practice monitoring and adjusting your nonverbal cues appropriately and pay greater attention to other people's body language to better understand them.*

Now we're on to a skill that doesn't really sound like it's a skill at all, but it is, and it's one of the most valuable skills you can practice to better connect with anyone—listening.

Chapter Six

HEAR ME OUT
(ACTIVE LISTENING)

If listening is something humans do naturally, why have I devoted an entire chapter to active listening? Although humans do hear things naturally, whether they actually listen with the intent of understanding and connecting with someone is an entirely different skill. Yes, that's right—skill. The skill of active listening is one of the fundamental components of building better relationships.

Hear Me Out Scenario

"Indi, I need to tell you something. It's kind of hard to say, but I need to tell you because I don't know who else I can tell."

Indi stops writing and looks at Chloe and thinks, *Wow, Chloe has barely spoken to me all semester. What's got her wanting to open up to her science lab partner now?* "Um, okay. Sure," she says and glances away.

It's clear by Chloe's body language that she is uncomfortable with whatever she is about to say. "Well, I know it sounds silly, but it really matters to me." Chloe pauses for a moment and takes a deep breath.

Indi shifts uncomfortably in her seat and quickly says, "Yes, and? You can just say it already, this class doesn't go all day."

Choe gazes down at the table and says, "Oh, it's just I heard someone in my group was spreading rumors about me that totally aren't true, and this morning I found out there's a party this weekend that I wasn't invited to, and I just . . ." When she looks up, she sees that Indi's texting beneath the table.

"Indi?"

"Oh, yep, sorry. My boyfriend just texted me. He really is just the sweetest. Anyway, yes, you were saying that your friends invited you to a party this weekend?"

"Well, no, that's not what I said."

"Do you know where that party's at? My boyfriend might actually be invited, too." Indi quickly starts texting away again trying to find out.

"I actually said I'm *not* invited to the party, and since you're not part of that group, I was wondering if you would want to—"

"Ask them if they'll invite you?" Indi interrupts. "Look, that isn't my place, and I don't think that's a good idea. Plus, I'm the nerdy kid no one really listens to anyway. So how about we just keep it as us being science partners and leave it at that."

Indi starts to shuffle through her papers because she feels so awkward talking about friendships. She just wants this conversation to be over.

Chloe feels a hot wave of shame rush over her body. She was actually going to ask Indi if she wanted to hang out and go to the movies this weekend, but she feels like Indi didn't listen to a word she'd said.

WHAT IS ACTIVE LISTENING?

It may seem strange to think of listening as a skill and probably sounds even stranger to see the word *active* in front of it—like, are we talking about listening while you're taking a jog or running around? Nope, we are talking about being completely present and focused when someone is speaking so you are not only hearing but actually understanding and connecting with what they are saying.

Active listening is incredibly important for the health of your friendships and other relationships. If you don't make an effort to purposely listen to your family and friends, there can be a lot of misunderstandings, tension, and unnecessary arguments. Think of how many times you've ended up in a fight with your mom because you were texting and not listening when she asked you a question, or when you showed up late for team practice because you weren't listening when your coach said be early.

In a world with so many distractions (especially our phones!) and all the thoughts racing through your head, it's easy to simply "hear" someone without actually listening to them. Learning how to actively listen with sincere interest is a skill that takes practice, but the payoff is worth it; it can help improve your relationships and ability to connect with others. Let's take a look at the key principles of active listening followed by some helpful strategies to build this skill.

Don't Interrupt

When someone is saying something that you don't necessarily agree with or something you know a lot about, it can be tempting to cut them short and interrupt. But how do you feel when someone interrupts you when you're trying to explain or express something? Yeah, not awesome, I bet. Interrupting someone mid-conversation can make people feel disrespected and as if what they have to say doesn't matter. Even if you don't mean it that way, it can still come across like that.

We tend to interrupt others when we're already planning what we want to say back to them while they're still talking. You may be so focused on mentally planning your counterargument or next question that you might as well be a million miles away, because your mind certainly is. Once you bring it back to the moment, you just blurt out what you want to say, and the other person feels totally disregarded—the opposite of what you want someone to feel if you're trying to build a friendship with them or improve your relationship. Disrespecting someone's point of view won't help them respect yours. The key to better active listening is to actually listen more and interrupt less.

Ask Questions

Many students I coach think that asking questions makes them look like they don't know anything. That's not true. Asking questions during a conversation actually shows you do know something—what that person is talking about! You can only ask a relevant question if you've been listening and know what they're actually talking about.

The key word here is *relevant*. If someone is telling you how stressed they are about finals, asking them, "How long do elephants usually live?" is completely irrelevant. You want to ask questions about them or the specific topic they're talking about to show that you are interested and care about what they're saying.

Letting someone talk away to you and not bothering to ask them questions won't help you seem cooler or smarter. Rather, it may very well be interpreted as a lack of interest in what they are saying, which is definitely not the best way to build connections in social situations.

Show You're Listening

If you're like most teens, your mom or dad has gotten frustrated with you and said, "Are you even listening to me?!" Whether you had your head turned away looking out the passenger window or you were fussing with your hair in the mirror, they were asking if you were listening because you weren't *showing* signs that you were. With your attention focused elsewhere, a lack of eye contact, and no affirming replies or questions, it's no surprise the other person feels like their message is being ignored. The good news is that there are plenty of subtle yet important ways to show someone you are indeed listening and understand what they're saying.

Mirror

Mirroring, also known as reflective listening, involves verbally reflecting back words to the speaker, showing them their message is being heard and received by you. In a sense, you become their mirror. Now please note I didn't say, "Become their parrot," and repeat word-for-word every single thing they say. Mirroring is about paraphrasing the underlying meaning and emotion they're trying to convey through their words.

You don't have to agree with someone's perspective to mirror it. You can disagree with what they're saying but still use mirroring to let them know that what they've said hasn't just gone in one ear and out the other. For example, if your friend says, "I can't believe you didn't ask if I wanted to come out with the group last weekend!" instead of immediately getting defensive, you could employ mirroring and say, "You're upset you didn't get to come on Saturday night. You would've liked to join us."

The key to effective mirroring is to avoid adding your own opinion to the message. Although it is difficult, to keep the conversation free of conflict, you'll want to remain open-minded and free of judgment.

Don't Be a Thought-Grabber

If someone is in the middle of speaking and you feel the temptation to interrupt, whether out of excitement, boredom, or frustration, remind yourself not to be a thought-grabber. Interrupting someone mid-sentence can steal away their train of thought, making them forget what they were saying. Instead, show everyone the respect they deserve; let them finish getting all their thoughts out and then share your thoughts.

Nothing good comes from interrupting someone. Think about how it feels when you get cut off before you finish what you want or need to say. If you don't like when it happens to you, be the change you want to see in the world, and don't interrupt.

Get Curious and Ask Questions

A great way to show someone you're listening is to ask follow-up questions about what they're saying. It says, "I hear you and want to know more about what you're telling me." There's no one-size-fits-all question because it depends on the context of what they're talking about. But here are a few of my favorite questions that I use often in conversation and you can try next time:

- *Can you tell me more about that?*

- *What is it about this that matters most to you?*

- *Is there anything else you want to add?*

- *What's the thing you really want me to understand about this?*

- *So now that* (insert their event/concern) *has happened, what do you think is the best thing to do next?*

Remember, you don't have to know what to ask someone ahead of time. When you're genuinely interested in hearing what they have to say, you will find the questions will come naturally from your own curiosity and care. So just remind yourself that.

Seeing Is Believing: Show You're Listening

There's a reason your parents get frustrated when you're scrolling on your phone when they're talking to you: It looks like you're not paying attention to what they're saying (and let's be honest, you probably aren't!). Happy and strong relationships require active listening.

Even if you think you can multitask—look at the TV or play with your hair—while someone is speaking to you, make it your mission to not just know in your head that you're listening but show them. Give them your undivided attention just like you prefer people give to you. Help them see that you're listening through your verbal and nonverbal cues:

- Look at who you're talking to and maintain comfortable eye contact throughout the conversation.

- Nod your head every so often to show your interest and that you understand what they're saying.

- Make appropriate affirming comments after they take a slight pause from what they're saying, such as "Oh, okay, I see," or "I get what you mean," or "That must have been hard/exciting/worrying," and so on.

Be Where Your Feet Are

Sometimes you may find that it's easy to get lost in your own thoughts or get distracted by something near you like your phone, TV, clothing, someone else nearby, etc. Whatever the distraction, it's easy to be a million miles away from the person who's speaking even if they are right in front of you.

One of my favorite sayings to bring myself back to the present moment is "Be where your feet are." Don't worry about dinner, whether you'll be invited to that party, or the text message you want to reply to. Keep your mind focused on where your feet are, which is right next to the person who's speaking. Ground yourself in that moment and give them your full attention. Your thoughts may be important, but so is the person talking to you.

Silence Speaks

Awkward silences, we've all had them before, right? It's that silence after someone finishes speaking and you're not sure what to say and it feels like it drags on for days. Well, here's the good news: There's no such thing as "awkward" silence. It's just a period of time when no one is talking, and what makes it awkward is that you're thinking, *Quick, this is so weird. Think of something! Ah crap I don't know what to say!* Before you know it, you blurt out something totally random.

Silence itself isn't awkward; it just is—especially when someone is sharing their thoughts with you. Sometimes that space of no noise or words is exactly what that person needs to process more of their thoughts and emotions. If you're always jumping in to fill that silence, you're taking away their ability to self-reflect and express themselves. Leave room for silence, knowing it's a healthy part of conversations.

Now, if the conversation has naturally wound down and you're not sure what to say next, try the strategies "Get Curious and Ask Questions" on page 86 and "Elephant in the Room" on page 37.

Be the Mirror, Not the Judge

As we discussed, mirroring is reflecting back to someone the message you heard them say, but in your own words and without judgment. That means leaving out critical statements like "I can't believe you just said that!" and using statements like "From what I heard, you believe..." or "From my understanding, I get the feeling that..."

If your coach is chatting with you after a game and says, "I need you to be more involved in the play and stop hanging at the back so much," you may be tempted to judge what he said, and say, "Are you telling me I don't deserve a spot on the team?" However, the far more useful choice is to mirror what he just said and say, "Okay, so you want me to be more hands-on because you see I have more to give." This way, you clearly communicate that you "get" what he means without adding your own meaning to his words. It's less defensive and judgmental, so it's less likely to turn into a disagreement or conflict, right? When it comes to mirroring, don't try to change the reflection—*be* the reflection.

Listen to Understand, Not to Respond

Without even realizing it, many of us listen to someone speak but don't pay attention to what they're saying because we're too busy thinking about what we're going to say next. This tends to happen most often when we're arguing with someone or when we're feeling nervous meeting new people. The problem is, when you're all up in your own head planning how you're going to respond, you often end up feeling lost in the conversation. When you haven't been listening properly or have been too busy judging what they're saying, you miss the underlying message or emotion in their words. That's how you end up in a misunderstanding or conflict.

The key is to let someone talk and listen to the meaning in their words instead of planning the big response in your head while they're speaking. Your only job is to "hold the space" for them. You're not trying to squash them, change them, or fix them. You are listening to their thoughts, fears, and emotions and simply letting them be. That's the foundation of true connection and understanding in relationships.

Hear Me Out Scenario Redux

"Indi, I need to tell you something. It's kind of hard to say, but I need to tell you because I don't know who else I can tell."

Indi stops writing and looks at Chloe. *Okay, this is different*, Indi thinks. *Chloe doesn't usually speak to me much. I wonder what's on her mind.* "Sure, Chloe, what's up?" Indi asks, drops her pen, and turns her attention toward Chloe with a curious smile on her face. She notices that Chloe is uncomfortable with what she's about to say.

"Well, I know it sounds silly, but it really matters to me . . ." Chloe pauses for a moment and takes a deep breath.

Indi looks at Chloe with a look of encouragement in her eyes. She knows it can be hard to speak up, so she just wants to give Chloe the time to process her thoughts.

Choe gazes down at the table and says, "I've found out someone in my group was spreading rumors about me that totally aren't true, and this morning I found out there's a party this weekend that I wasn't invited to. Everything was fine, but the last few weeks they've turned on me."

Chloe looks up to meet eyes with Indi, who's slowly nodding.

"Oh, Chloe, that's a tough situation. How are you feeling?" Indi asks.

"Pretty embarrassed, I guess," Chloe mumbles quietly.

"Yeah, that's understandable. What about it is most upsetting to you?"

"Feeling like no one likes me anymore. Well, at least not anyone in that group, and so I was just wondering if . . ." Chloe pauses again and looks to the ground and then back to Indi.

Indi lets Chloe take a moment to compose herself.

"We've been science partners for a while now, but we don't really know each other that well yet, so I was wondering if you'd want to hang out together this weekend? Maybe see a movie or something?"

Indi breaks into a smile. "You know what, that sounds really fun actually! I just have to check with my mom to make sure we don't have any plans, but other than that, I'm in!"

Chloe's eyes light up as she smiles back at Indi. Perhaps she isn't quite as alone in this world as she thought.

The MORE YOU KNOW

Given that this chapter is all about listening, here's a fun fact: 55 percent of our day is spent doing some form of listening, but we're only likely to retain about 17 to 25 percent of what we hear. You know how your teachers say to take notes when they're talking to the class? That's why. Your brain isn't as great at remembering things as you give it credit for, but active listening is one way you can definitely improve the chances of accurately recalling what someone said!

TAKEAWAYS

Active listening doesn't just happen; it takes practice. Here are some key points to keep in mind:

- *Active listening is more than just hearing someone; it's deliberately paying attention to what they're saying and making an effort to understand the message and emotion conveyed in their words.*

- *Purposely listening to your family and friends can help reduce misunderstandings, tension, and unnecessary arguments and build better connections.*

- *Resisting the urge to interrupt, listening to understand, remaining judgment-free, staying present, allowing space for silence, and asking questions are all powerful skills to practice.*

Active listening is good, but when paired with empathy, it's even better. That's why the next chapter dives into the skill of empathy and explores why the happiest relationships in the world are built upon being able to empathize with others.

I FEEL YOU

(EMPATHY)

In a world where it's easy to judge and crit-
icize others, empathy is a skill that brings
out the best in humanity. Practicing empathy
means practicing patience, compassion, love,
and understanding. It means thinking beyond
yourself and stepping into someone else's
shoes. It's what creates lasting relationships
and true friendships—the kind that can
weather the bad days as well as the good.
This chapter teaches you how to become
more empathetic to improve your relationships with others—and yourself.

Empathy Scenario

Katie is anxiously sitting at her desk, staring at yet another math equation that doesn't make any sense.

Why am I so stupid? I'm going to screw up my math exam yet again, she thinks with frustrated tears in her eyes.

As she scribbles on the page, she hears footsteps coming and in bursts her older sister, Nicole, like a freight train. Nicole is full of energy and excitement for the night out she's about to have with her friends for her birthday.

"Hey, Katie! How's it going?" Nicole says with a big smile on her face while walking toward Katie's wardrobe.

Katie tenses up and slowly looks over to Nicole with a nasty look on her face. "Seriously, Nicole?! How selfish are you just barging into my room like that? Can't you see I'm trying to study here?!" Katie rolls her eyes in disgust and stares down at her math book.

"Oh, come on, Katie, lighten up. I promise I'll only be a minute. I'm just wondering if I can borrow your jeans for tonight," Nicole says as she opens the sliding door to Katie's wardrobe.

"Um, don't you have your own jeans? Why do you always have to wear mine?! Anyway, I'm sick of you always coming into my room without asking. I have an exam on Monday and all you ever think of is yourself!"

Nicole stops and turns to face Katie. "Oh . . ." Her face falls a little and her eyes go to the ground.

Nicole wasn't meaning to be rude; she was just excited for her birthday and wanted to share the excitement with her sister.

"I didn't mean to make you think I don't care about your exam, Katie," she says, "I'm always proud of how hard you work. I just wanted to borrow your jeans—that's all."

"Yeah, well, maybe you should've thought of that before you just came barging into my room and interrupting me. Just get out, okay?"

"Oh, um, okay, sorry." Nicole closes the wardrobe and slowly walks out of the room, with tears in her eyes.

Katie sits there fuming with anger, but she's also ashamed of what she just said to her sister. She scrunches up her math paper, throws herself on the bed, and buries her head in her pillows to cry.

WHAT IS EMPATHY?

I dedicated this book to my older sister, Nicole. She was the most wonderful, kind, and fun-loving human who I looked up to from the day I was born. But, sometimes, by the way I treated and spoke to her, you wouldn't have known it. The scenario you just read is actually a real-life story between my sister and me. (She always called me Katie, and I loved it.)

You can hear how quick I was to jump down her throat and be mean to her. At the time, I felt justified in doing so. I thought what mattered more than taking a moment to understand my sister was getting the best grades and proving to everyone how smart I was. I was afraid of failing, but rather than taking a moment to reflect upon those fears, I acted them out on my sister.

A few years after I finished high school, my sister was killed in an accident. And now those grades matter so little to me. I wish I hadn't been so quick to rush Nicole out of my room when she'd come in to ask, "Katie, can I borrow your . . . ?" or tell me about her day because I was "too busy" getting whatever task done.

What I lacked in these moments with my sister was empathy: the ability to understand other people's emotions and think about things from their point of view, as well as taking a moment to rationalize my own. If you've ever heard your parents say, "Take a moment to stand in their shoes," that's exactly what empathy is. It's being able to recognize and respond to how someone is thinking and feeling. It's a skill that I definitely did not practice as a teenager in my relationships with family members. I learned the hard way how quickly life can change. Empathy is something I value as one of the most import-ant social skills of all.

If you are feeling overwhelmed by work or study right now, keep perspective. A few points less on your grade can't compare to a few minutes lost with someone you love. We tend to view our stresses as if they're never going to leave us and our loved ones as if they are always going to be there. When really the opposite is true: Your "storm" won't last forever, but neither will the person you love who's copping the full brunt of your stress. Kindness is always available to you, and it's always the best option, because one year from now, who knows where your life could be?

Let's look a little more deeply at what empathy is (and isn't) and then review some helpful ways you can start building this essential social skill.

Accepting Others' Emotions

"They shouldn't feel so frustrated!"

"They should be happier about what happened."

"They shouldn't cry so much."

Whenever we have thoughts about how someone "should" or "shouldn't" be, we are doing the opposite of being empathetic to their emotions—we are judging them. As soon as we judge someone for the way they're being and think we know better than they do, we disconnect from them. The answer to reconnecting with people and improving your relationships, whether it's with your family, teachers, or friends, is to accept how they're feeling in that moment. Even if it's not how you would react or feel in that situation, you need to accept that this is where they're at; this is how they're feeling. Whether they're feeling anxious, upset, excited, or jealous, people don't have to feel the way you think they should. Everyone is free to feel and act in any way they like.

It's tough to accept because unfortunately that means people may sometimes feel negatively toward you. However, if you can under-stand that it's okay for people to feel what they need to feel and stop trying to resist their emotions, you can reduce the frustration and resentment that can otherwise build up in friendships and other relationships.

Think about how many fights you've had with a friend who got monumentally upset because you didn't do something, and you just don't understand why or think she should be so upset—perhaps you didn't reply to her text or save her a seat in class. I've definitely been angry at people for overreacting, but then I just end up overreacting back at them. Now I'm doing exactly what I'm judging them for, and more often than not, it leads to further misunderstandings and frustrations.

There's simply no upside to judging people for how they feel. However, you gain so much peace and connection by accepting how others feel. Instead of getting upset at your friend's anger, take a moment to pause, breathe, and accept that it's okay they feel that way. There's no right or wrong way for someone to feel; they just feel their way. As a human being on this planet, their best way of coping with the situation at hand is to feel exactly how they're feeling—and that's okay.

This doesn't mean you disregard your own feelings in that moment, either. It means recognizing that everyone's feelings matter, and you don't need to try to control or change them. In fact, you can't. Remember, it's not the circumstances producing their feelings, but what they're thinking and how they're interpreting what's happening. You don't have the power to control someone else's brain. You do have the ability to "step inside someone's mind" and consider their perspective to better understand what could be causing them to react that way. This leads us to the next important piece of empathy: perspective-taking.

Perspective-Taking

"I can't believe they're being so unreasonable."

"I don't get why they're being so quiet."

"I only said that because he was being such a jerk."

Empathy is not only showing consideration for *how* someone feels but also considering *why* they feel that way. That means thinking about how they are seeing things from their point of view.

Think of it like this: You're sitting on the left side of the bus going to school, and your friend is on the right side. Even though you're on the same bus going to the same destination, you are seeing different things along the way because you have different perspectives from inside the bus. Your friend may say, "Hey, did you see the cute dog walking on the sidewalk?" and you totally missed it because it was outside your perspective. Meanwhile, he missed the break dancer on your side of the street.

In this example, you and your friend won't see the exact same thing because there are things blocking your unique perspective. In real life, the things blocking our ability to see someone else's point of view are judgment and righteousness. Righteousness is the idea that we always know best, what we believe is right, and what they think is wrong. The truth is, there are no right or wrong perspectives; there are just different perspectives. Everyone's perspective is affected by a range of things, including their upbringing, past experiences, values, and personality types.

Instead of trying to prove you're right and they're wrong (because there's no objective winner to that anyway!), I encourage you to shift your focus and try to better understand their perspective from a genuine place of curiosity rather than criticism. You can do this by replacing the thought, *I can't believe they're doing that!* with, *Why are they reacting like this?*

For example, your parents may say that you can't go out with your friends one night. You immediately judge them as being unfair and trying to control you. So, you lash out and say nasty things to try to get them to let you go. Now guess what you're doing: You are attempting to control them in return. It's a power play neither of you is going to win. In the end, you're both angry, frustrated, and not speaking to each other for the rest of the weekend. Again, can you see how there are no winners?

Instead, what if your parents say you can't go out with your friends and you don't immediately judge their decision as unfair and a way of trying to control you? Instead, what if you pause and drop into that space of "They're Doing the Best They Can" (see page 62)? Then ask yourself, "How can I see that they're doing the best they can right now?" Think about that outcome and how there might be less anger, tension, and frustration.

Realistically, I'm sure your parents aren't waking up each morning thinking about how they can ruin your day. In fact, a parent's natural instinct is to protect you from potential harm. It's scary for them to see you growing up and making your own decisions. Even though they realize they need to allow you space to sometimes make mistakes, their first instinct is always going to be to protect you. It's not because they don't trust you—they don't trust the world. They've seen things you haven't. And their "doing their best right now" includes not letting you go to certain parties or grounding you if you argue back.

By taking a moment to explain their point of view, I may not have eliminated your judgmental thoughts entirely, but do you feel a little less frustrated and a little more accepting of their decision? Typically, the answer I hear from the teens I coach is yes.

Also, I want to remind you that staying angry at someone for what they've done or how they're reacting doesn't punish them—it only punishes you. The other person doesn't feel your feelings, only you do. We all know that feeling frustrated, judgmental, and critical doesn't feel great. Feelings of acceptance, understanding, and compassion feel a whole lot better, right? Feeling greater empathy for someone's point of view is a gift not only for others but also for yourself. You can find so much relief and freedom when you value other people's perspectives as much as your own.

Human beings are complicated and messy creatures with so much going on in our internal worlds that we don't always show up as our best. We often have no idea what someone has gone through in life, which affects what they think and how they react to things. But choosing to believe people are always coming from a well-intentioned place is a powerful step to diffusing conflict and building connection in any given situation.

Be the Change

The number-one thing that helps me drop into a place of empathy is reminding myself to "Be the change you want to see." By that I mean, if you are constantly criticizing others for being so negative or judgmental, you are being negative or judgmental right back, which only adds to the negativity and judgment in the world—the very thing we're outraged against!

To break this toxic cycle, each and every one of us needs to step up and be the change we want to see! Make "Be the change" your mantra to remind yourself to give the same level of patience and understanding to others that you wish they would give to you when you're letting your fears or insecurities get the better of you. Be the change you want to see by choosing compassion.

No One Is Ever Less-Than

You know that "friend" who started a rumor about you on a group chat or that ex who cheated on you? As much as you want to tear them down, the truth is they are no less valuable as a human being than you are. As humans, our worth is inherent. That doesn't mean you never set boundaries or continue to be friends with that person. It does mean that you take action from a place of understanding that their actions don't make you or them less worthy.

No one is better than someone else. We're all just different humans having different life experiences. One way you can begin to help someone stop acting from that fearful place is to remember that everyone is worthy of empathy and understanding.

Step into Their Shoes (*What If That Had Been Me?*)

An easy way to practice empathy is to choose one sad news story every day and simply ask yourself, "How would I feel if that happened to me?"

As someone whose family tragedy did end up in the news when I lost my sister, I know firsthand those stories aren't just statistics or another news grab. They are real people just like you with families who love them and future dreams that won't get to come true.

You don't have to go through an awful experience yourself to show compassion for the suffering in the world. It takes great strength to practice the humility to show up for others from a more open and gentler place. So, although you want to be mindful not to spend all day losing yourself in sad news, it can be powerful to take a moment to read someone's story and ask yourself, "What if that had been me or my family?"

Rather than breeze right by these stories, take a moment to stop what you're doing, mentally visualize standing in their shoes, and think about how you would feel if you'd been through a similar tragic experience. Allow the sadness, compassion, or sorrow to flow through your body and send love to the person experiencing sadness and tragedy—I can guarantee they need it.

Curiosity over Criticism

The next time someone does something that makes you want to scream, "I just don't understand why you would do that?!", hit your internal pause button and flip the question to, "What's one well-intentioned reason they may have done that?" This immediately takes you from criticizing someone to getting curious about them. This will help you feel less frustrated and therefore be less short-tempered with them, which is a huge part of diffusing conflict and potential arguments.

People can tell when they are being judged or criticized, and it makes them defensive and want to attack back. But if you ask them in a curious, soft tone of voice, "Hey, what's really going on here? Is there something more to this that I don't understand?" they're far more likely to respond in a softer, less defensive way. This means you're likely to move into a genuine conversation where real feelings and thoughts are safe to come to the surface. This usually leads to more understanding and conflict resolution.

Once you learn someone's point of view or listen to more of why they're feeling a certain way, you may realize you might have reacted in a similar way if you had the same beliefs or experiences. Even if it's not the perspective you normally take, try on their point of view and see how it's not as unfair or irrational as you initially thought.

Remember, curiosity opens up connection, whereas criticism shuts it down. Choosing to be curious before being critical will help you out every time.

Journal Your Heart Out

If you're really worked up about something and you just can't quite get to a place of curiosity and compassion for someone, instead of trying to do it all in your mind, grab a piece of paper or your journal. Work through the thoughts and judgments that are holding you back by answering these key questions:

1. What am I thinking about what this person said or did that's really causing how I feel right now? (For example, *they're so unfair, they're jerks, they're irrational, they're selfish,* etc.)

2. If I was my most fair and understanding self, what else could I make their feelings or actions mean?

3. If I knew their reaction was triggered by past hurt or a fear that they're not good enough (because trust me, it likely is coming from that!), how would I react differently? What would I be thinking instead?

4. In what way is my reaction and judgment triggered by past hurt or a fear that I'm not good enough? How would I react differently if I didn't let this hurt or insecurity be in charge of my response?

5. When have I reacted in a similar way and what did I need from the other person? Was it more judgment or more understanding?

6. What if I choose to love myself and the other person and let us both be humans who struggle sometimes? From this perspective, what would I say to them if they were in front of me right now?

Take a moment to read your answers and pick the one that feels most true to you and helps you show up as the kind of person you want to be. Then call that person or go see them and tell them! It's the choice that feels best for them and for you.

Hurt People Hurt People

You may have heard this saying before: "Hurt people hurt people." It's one of my favorite sayings when it comes to building empathy, especially when you're really struggling to understand how someone can be so cruel. Honestly, think about when you feel really good and confident in yourself. You don't go around criticizing your friend's profile picture or making fun of someone's new job. When you feel insecure or fearful that you're not enough the way you are, you're more likely to lash out and put others down. And those insecurities often come from past hurts we haven't yet healed, like someone bullying us or our parents mistreating us.

Insecurities never come from a good place, and they never lead us to one. Unfortunately, people often let their insecurities drive their reactions, not because they want to, but because they don't know any better. But you do. You now understand that "hurt people hurt people," so you can sink into a place of compassion rather than hate for them—because hate has never healed someone's hurt, but empathy always can.

Think of Your Legacy

So far I've focused on showing empathy in situations where people may be feeling frustrated or saying something unkind about you, but you can show empathy in day-to-day interactions, like the one with my sister, when I failed to think about how my crankiness could be coming across to her. She walked into my room excited and left feeling dejected. That's the last thing I wanted, but I let my ego and insecurities get in the way. I look back on that with such regret. And although I can't turn back time and change what I said, I can ensure I don't repeat the cycle of lashing out because of my insecurities. In fact, my mantra in life is "Leave people better than I found them."

I encourage you to take on the same mantra in your life. Each and every one of us is only here for a finite time, and the way we treat others becomes the legacy we leave behind. Leave a legacy you are proud of by choosing kindness every time.

Empathy Scenario Redux

Katie is anxiously sitting at her desk, staring at yet another math equation that doesn't make any sense.

This is so hard. I don't know why I bother sometimes, she thinks while scribbling on the page and blinking back tears of frustration.

She hears footsteps coming and in bursts her older sister, Nicole, who is a naturally loud and energetic person. It's Nicole's birthday, but Katie is not in the mood for a conversation with her right now.

"Hey, Katie! How's it going?" Nicole asks with a big smile on her face while walking toward Katie's wardrobe.

Katie tenses up, and her instinct is to yell at her sister to get out, but she pauses for a moment and thinks, *Okay, think about if it was my birthday and I was super excited about it. I'd likely be loud and not notice what someone else was working on, either. I'm sure she's not doing this just to be annoying. So just breathe for a moment and find out what she's after.*

"Hey, Nickers. What's up?" Katie asks, putting her pen down and turning to smile at Nicole, while thinking, *Be the change. Be calm and kind. There's no upside to getting cranky right now.*

"I know you're studying at the moment so I'm sorry for interrupting, but have you seen your light blue jeans? I'd love to borrow them for tonight!" Nicole says while opening Katie's wardrobe.

Katie briefly smiles at her sister's apology. *I guess it's true,* she thinks. *If you take a moment to see things from someone else's perspective, it will often inspire them to do the same.*

"That's okay, Nicole. I do have a lot of studying, but I know you won't keep me long. Those jeans will look great on you tonight, but I think they're actually in the wash," Katie says as she walks toward her wardrobe.

"Oh . . ." Nicole's face looks crestfallen, and Katie feels the disappointment in her heart. She knows Nicole loves to feel pretty on her birthday, and she knows what it's like when the outfit you planned on doesn't work out.

continued →

"Yeah, I hate when that happens. But, hey, it's okay! Maybe these jeans go well with your top as well? Why not try these on?" Katie reaches in and pulls out her favorite pair of white jeans.

Nicole looks at Katie with wide eyes and says, "Oh, you know what? You're so right! I think the white will actually look amazing with my red top! Thanks, Katie, you're the best!" Nicole squeezes her little sister before rushing out of the room to try on the jeans.

Katie chuckles to herself and feels a warm-fuzzy feeling flow through her body for helping make her sister's day, simply by showing empathy.

I should practice this more often, Katie thinks as she picks up her pen with a little smile on her face and renewed energy to sit down and concentrate on figuring out the next math equation.

The MORE YOU KNOW

It's wonderful that you've read this chapter on empathy, because the world needs more of it right now: A 2010 study from the University of Michigan found that the average American college student in 2009 was less empathetic than 75 percent of students in 1979—and the study was more than a decade ago. So basically, empathy is on the decline. I hope what you've read in this chapter inspires you to "be the change" so we can see empathy back on the rise again!

TAKEAWAYS

As with every other skill, you can improve your ability to be empathetic with practice. Remember these key points:

- Before you judge others, take a moment to consider their point of view and why they may be reacting that way from a place of curiosity rather than from a critical perspective.

- Empathy is the thread that weaves together true understanding and connection in relationships. The more we give, the more we are able to solve conflicts and heal past hurts—for ourselves and others.

- Your "storms" won't last forever, but neither will the person who's taking the brunt of them. So choose kindness every time.

Now that we've been through a big overview of social skills, it's time to get down to the nitty-gritty and put what you've learned into practice in your daily life.

Chapter Eight

GET ON IT
(PUTTING SKILLS INTO ACTION)

So far, this book has been like a plane, flying up in the sky to give you the bird's-eye view of all the different skills that come together to help you feel calmer and more confident in social situations. Now I'm going to land the plane in a few different socially challenging situations and explain which of these skills are most important to help you handle similar circumstances in a healthy way.

Up for Criticism

"Don't swing so hard at the ball," Coach yells from the other side of the net.

Jeremy looks across the court at his coach and slams his tennis racquet to the ground. "This is a stupid game anyway!" he yells back, kicking the tennis ball into the fence.

He didn't want to take tennis lessons, but his dad wanted him to give it a try. Now he wishes he'd refused to get out of the car.

"It's okay, Jeremy. A lot of people struggle to get the hang of their forehand. It'll take some practice, but you'll get there," Coach says, trying to get Jeremy's attention back.

The coach is already annoyed with the mini tantrum Jeremy is throwing, but he tries to stay calm. He realizes Jeremy is probably just nervous, so it's natural he's acting out a little.

"I'd rather throw these balls than play this dumb game and listen to you," Jeremy says, as he throws a few balls as hard as he can.

"Excuse me, Jeremy? I'm okay with you being upset, but I'm not okay with being disrespected on my own court—"

"Whatever," Jeremy interrupts. "I'm not being rude, you're being rude. I'm out of here."

Jeremy stomps off the court, knowing his dad won't let him play video games tonight because of this. But he can't help it. As soon as someone criticizes him, they've crossed a line.

PRACTICE YOUR SKILLS

Being defensive is often our automatic response when someone criticizes us or tries to give us constructive feedback. We immediately want to defend ourselves or lash out because we take it as a personal attack. The truth is, whether it's someone giving you feedback on your tennis swing or what you're wearing, you don't have to take it personally—because it's not personal. They're simply sharing their thoughts, opinions, or beliefs—some may be helpful, and others won't be. Most people offer feedback or criticism out of a genuine desire to see you improve or because putting others down makes them feel better. What they say has nothing to do with your value as a human, so don't take it that way. If you don't agree with what they're saying, you can still allow space for their opinion. Everyone is entitled to their own thoughts and beliefs.

Consider criticism or constructive feedback as information you can either learn from or let go of. To figure out which it is, ask yourself two questions:

1. Is there any truth in what they're saying that I can use to better myself? (Maybe your friend says you're being selfish. Take a moment to reflect. Could that be true? Are you proud of your actions or is there something you'd like to change?)

2. Is this person speaking from their own insecurities to try to make me feel insecure?

The key to accepting criticism is choosing to interpret feedback as a chance to learn something new. When you take on this interpretation, there's no need to get defensive. When you get defensive, you miss the opportunity to find the lesson. Staying open and curious—and knowing you're an amazing human being no matter what—is the key to learning from criticism in an empowering way.

☑ *Emotional Intelligence*

Too often we use someone's opinion as a reason to shame ourselves. But the truth is, other people's words don't have the power to hurt your feelings. Only you can do that when you allow their words to define your worthiness or abilities. Using your emotional intelligence when receiving criticism and feedback will help you remember it's not about what that person said but how you interpreted it.

This is an important distinction because it puts the power back in your hands to manage how you feel without getting defensive. The PAC strategy will help you focus on what you do have control over: challenging your own thoughts and beliefs in that moment rather than someone else's. By challenging whatever negative thought you're attaching to their feedback, you'll feel less embarrassed and more confident.

Want to practice this skill more? Check out "Don't React, PAC (Pause, Ask, and Challenge)" on page 60, "Take Off Your 'Skepticals'" on page 59, and "My Best Self" on page 61.

☑ *Confidence*

You may recall from chapter 3 that one of the keys to true confidence is knowing your value as a human being is never on the line—ever. This is important to remember when receiving criticism, because we often take someone's opinion of us and use it to define our "enough-ness." This is where you need to remind yourself that there are always going to be people who see things differently than you do, and that's okay. It's also okay that someone may be more skilled at something than you are. That doesn't make them better than you.

Let's piece that skill together with your understanding of a growth mindset, which we discussed on page 24—that your abilities aren't a fixed trait but something you can improve upon. Having someone tell you how you can improve your tennis swing or solve the math equation correctly is necessary feedback to help you grow. Remind yourself that "feedback is your friend" and is always on your side if you choose to find the value in it.

Want to practice this in your life? Check out "Peaches and Preferences" on page 37 and "The Rule of Three" on page 39.

☑ *Active Listening*

When someone is giving you constructive feedback, there's a temptation to shut down and stop listening. That only creates tension, and you miss out on the lesson they're sharing. By getting defensive rather than listening to his coach, Jeremy missed out on improving his tennis swing and turned it into a heated argument.

People are also likely to get frustrated if they feel like their feedback is being ignored. For example, perhaps your mom is explaining how she'd like you to give her more notice when you need to be picked up from a friend's place. If you're playing on your phone, she's likely going to get annoyed and repeat herself with a raised voice, right? But if you put your phone down and look at her to show you are actually listening, her feedback remains nothing more than a calm conversation because your mom feels heard and respected.

Even if you don't agree with someone's perspective, you should still respect that they're a human entitled to their own point of view. Whether you want to learn from it or let it go is up to you, but the only way to truly know the answer to that is to actively listen to their feedback—you can't learn from what you don't listen to.

Want to practice your active listening skills some more? Check out "Be the Mirror, Not the Judge" on page 88 and "Listen to Understand, Not to Respond" on page 89.

Handling Conflict

"Hey, Mom?!" Mia yells as she's looking for her mom in the house. She hears rustling in the laundry room, so she goes racing in.

"Yes, Mia, what is it?" her mom asks as she loads the washing machine.

"Kayla invited me over with Angie tonight. What time can you drop me off?" Mia asks, phone in hand, ready to text Kayla what time she'll get to her place.

With an apologetic look in her eye, Mia's mom says, "Oh, Mia, you know you're not allowed sleepovers the weekend before exam week. You never get any sleep and always come home cranky and tired. These are your first high school exams, and we want you to give your best. Any other weekend would be okay, but I'm sorry, not tonight, honey."

"What? Are you kidding me? You are SO unfair and controlling. I swear all you try to do is ruin my life and make me have no friends!"

"Whoa, hang on a second—"

"All I want to do is see my friends and all you want to do is control me. What is wrong with you?!" Mia shouts.

"Excuse me? You know these are the rules whether you like them or not. Part of growing up is learning how to respect them. I'm sorry, but no amount of nagging is going to get me to change my mind," her mom says, and then turns back to loading the washing machine.

Mia's eyes well with tears, and she yells, "Why did I have to get you as my mom? You NEVER let me do what I want to do. I hate you!"

Mia runs out of the laundry room, slamming the door, as her words deeply pierce her mom's heart.

PRACTICE YOUR SKILLS

Whether you find out a friend has spread a rumor about you, your coach drops you from the team, or your parents ground you for staying out too late, conflict and differences in perspective are part of life. But whether that conflict turns nasty and escalates into an emotional meltdown—or evolves into a healthy discussion and collaboration—is entirely up to you.

We become highly emotional in conflict when we slip into a place of blame, entitlement, and taking things personally. But by practicing a combination of the social skills we've explored, you can learn to respond to conflict in a way that helps you keep your emotions under control. This will help you have a real conversation with an open mind, allowing you to come to a solution together, rather than creating more conflict and tension.

The teens I coach often say, "I hate confrontation." Instead of becoming emotional and angry in conflicts, they'd rather avoid the conflict entirely to "keep the peace." But is there really any peace with this approach? Although you might do or say something that doesn't feel right to you to avoid a conflict with someone, internally, you don't feel peace because you've gone against your values and goals. Truthfully, it leaves important things unsaid and often eats away at your own self-esteem because you continually put other people's needs before your own.

Now I'm not saying you always need to speak up about something you disagree with or dislike; sometimes there is power in simply letting something go. Like if you hear someone in the hall make a snide remark about you and you just keep walking—there is power in that.

The best way to know whether you're avoiding conflict from a place of strength or fear is to ask yourself, "Am I not speaking up right now because I'm scared of what someone might think if I do?" There is a way you can respect other people while still respecting yourself.

☑ *Empathy*

Empathy is the most important skill when it comes to not letting your emotions escalate out of control during conflicts. Put yourself in the other person's shoes before freaking out and immediately blaming them.

If Mia had taken a moment to pause and put herself in her mom's shoes, she might have sensed her mom was preoccupied with the laundry and probably wishing for some help—and not having more demands made of her. She might have also realized her mom was actually being reasonable by letting her stay over at a friend's house any weekend except exam weekend. To her mom, it wasn't about controlling Mia but allowing her freedom while helping her do her best at school.

There is a space between what you hear someone say and how you react to it, and that space is in your mind where you pause and ask, "How can I see that this person is really doing the best they can right now?" Parents and teachers are humans, too. They're not always going to get it right, but being unkind toward them doesn't make us right, either. Be the change you want to see by choosing to stand in someone else's shoes rather than just throwing your shoes at them in frustration.

Want to keep practicing your empathy skills? Check out "Curiosity over Criticism" on page 103 and "Journal Your Heart Out" on page 104.

☑ *Active Listening*

Have you ever had an argument with someone and you're shouting at them so much you can't hear what they're actually saying? Yep. That's why conflicts can escalate quickly. Your brain is hijacked by stress hormones from the anger you're feeling caused by your judgment of the other person. At some point, you stop hearing what they're saying and focus on getting them to hear you. It's a lose-lose situation.

Resist the temptation to lose your mind, and instead feel empathy for them and remind yourself to hear them out. Listen to their concern from a place of wanting to understand, not just getting them to understand you. Show you're listening by uncrossing your arms and facing them with a relaxed posture. It's not always easy to do in heated moments, but it's worth the effort. Often people just need space to vent and express themselves, and if you listen with an empathetic ear, it can change everything.

If Mia had tried to understand that her mom thought exam week was important to her success, she may have said, "Mom, I know it's important that I study, and I want to do well, too. But my friends are important to me. Is there any way to meet in the middle?"

Who knows? Mia might have been able to hang with her friends till 9:00 p.m. instead of sitting in her room, angry at her mom for "ruining her night."

Ready to practice your active listening skills? Check out "Be Where Your Feet Are" on page 87 and "Don't Be a Thought-Grabber" on page 85.

☑ Emotional Intelligence

The number-one strategy that de-escalates conflict is knowing how to control your emotions in the heat of the moment and to stop the blame game. That's why emotional intelligence is powerful when paired with empathy and active listening.

As soon as you tell someone, "This is your fault," or "You're ruining everything," they will automatically respond by getting defensive. If someone says something like that to you, it doesn't exactly calm you down or make you want to listen to them, right? You can, however, practice your emotional intelligence—especially the PAC strategy— and take ownership of your emotions at any given moment.

Although Mia can't control her mom's decision, she *can* control her emotional outburst and all the anger she's feeling. Her mom isn't causing the anger and frustration. Those are a result of the thoughts that her mom shouldn't say no or that her mom is trying to control her. Of course these thoughts will turn into feelings of frustration and resentment, followed by aggressive body language and an angry tone of voice. This will likely escalate the tension.

Your parents, teachers, and friends are going to have their own beliefs and ways of doing things that may be different from yours, and that's okay. I want you to own the truth that you're still in control of your emotional reaction. Rather than letting anger automatically dictate your reaction, pause and intentionally choose how you want to feel about a circumstance you can't change. If you were to go beyond blame and negativity, how would your best self think and feel about this?

Want to practice increasing your emotional intelligence? Check out "My Best Self" on page 61, "Don't React, PAC (Pause, Ask and Challenge)" on page 60, "What's *Really* Causing How You Feel?" on page 57, and "They're Doing the Best They Can" on page 62.

Social Media: Keep It Locked

Ada checks her phone again. Still no reply. It's been four hours since she sent that message to Darron and three hours since he's read it. She can't believe he's left her on "read" with no response.

How embarrassing, she thinks. *No guy is ever going to like me.* She sighs as she closes Snapchat and opens Instagram. *Wow. Only three likes?! What's wrong with me? Why can't I be more like Mel?*

She taps on Mel's profile—a girl in her grade who has 1,700 more followers than she has—and sees that her latest photo has 23 comments—all of them saying how gorgeous she is.

Girls like me aren't cool enough and my thighs need to be way skinnier, Ada thinks, throwing her phone down on her bed and turning her face into the pillow.

Right then, her phone buzzes. Darron has replied! She opens Snapchat and sees a blank screen with one word: "hi."

She sinks back into her pillow, not sure which is worse: no reply or the world's lamest one? She hops up and looks in the mirror. *He's clearly not into me,* she thinks. *If only I was prettier and taller, and had a smaller nose.*

Little does Ada know that Darron thinks she's cool; he's just in the middle of a shift at work and is banned from using his phone on the floor. But when his boss wasn't looking, he snapped a quick blank photo and wrote "hi" to let her know he was thinking of her. Darron likes Ada, so she makes him nervous, and he's never sure what to say. Either way, he really hopes she replies.

PRACTICE YOUR SKILLS

Did you know that, on average, we laugh 15 times in a day, but we check our phones 150 times a day? Yes, we check our phones 10 times more often than we laugh each day! And that's just the beginning of a long list of crazy stats about teens, social media, and phone use. Did you know the average American teen spends seven hours a day on their phone and 41 percent of teens feel overwhelmed by the number of notifications they get every day? It's not just teens—even adults are becoming addicted to their phones. There's even a name for it: *nomophobia* (no-mobile-phone phobia)!

I'm not going to hate on social media and technology, because they make our lives better in so many ways. From video chatting with family across the world to making silly TikToks with our friends, there are many benefits that social media has brought into our daily lives. But there are also real downsides, especially when it comes to our social skills, self-esteem, and relationships. Although social media offers ease, speed, and convenience, it has taken away the quality of conversations because we are missing cues like body language, facial expressions, tone of voice, and eye contact. It's harder to feel empathy and concentrate on someone through a screen.

Let's now explore things to be mindful of when communicating via social media platforms and which skills it may be taking away from us. This will help remind you to make an effort to practice those skills as much as possible.

☑ *Empathy*

There are a few different ways to practice empathy when it comes to social media. First, consider how it comes across when you're playing on your phone in a social situation or when someone is trying to talk to you. It can leave them feeling like you don't respect or care about them. The next time you catch yourself scrolling on your phone while someone is talking to you—whether it's a teacher, friend, or sibling—remind yourself to bring your attention back to them. Give others the same consideration you like to receive. In fact, a great rule is to have no phones at the table, whether it's at lunch with friends or dinner with family. Watch how much more interesting the conversation gets when you're not distracted!

Another way to practice empathy with social media is to temper your expectations of how quickly someone "should" reply to a message. Think about how long you take to reply to someone. Usually, there's a reason that has zero to do with how you feel about them. Don't automatically assume someone doesn't care and get upset. Put yourself in their shoes and think about how you really don't know what's going on in their day. I'm sure you appreciate it when your friend doesn't get upset if you take a while to reply, so extend the same understanding. It makes for happier relationships when we do!

The final way we can practice empathy on social media is to remember that there is a human being on the other side of that screen. Be thoughtful of what you're saying; if you wouldn't say it to their face in person, don't say it at all.

Another great tool, originally created to combat cyberbullying, is the acronym THINK. Ask yourself the following:

Is it True? (Is it a fact or just your opinion or feeling?)

Is it Helpful? (Does it improve the situation?)

Is it Inspiring? (Does it uplift you, them, or the situation?)

Is it Necessary? (Is it worth bringing up? Will you worry about it in a few days?)

Is it Kind? (Is it coming from a place of care and goodwill?)

The THINK acronym helps bring back the best part of our humanness to conversations. No matter what platform you're using, that someone on the other end is a human being. So always THINK before you speak—or text.

Want more help practicing your empathy skills? Check out "No One Is Ever Less-Than" on page 102 and "Hurt People Hurt People" on page 105.

☑ *Confidence*

You are so much more than likes, views, comments, followers, and reshares. Your value as a human being isn't determined by any of these things. Your worth is absolute.

I know it feels very important to have a certain number of people liking your photos or sharing your videos, but the truth is—it's all just made up. According to Ignite Treatment Centers, 46 percent of teen girls in a study admitted feeling bad about themselves because of social media and the pressure they feel to live up to its unrealistic standards.

Let me clear something up: You do NOT have to live up to the standard of what you see online. Social media is the "reel life" that we control and manipulate with endless filters and recording options. But in "real life," we are human beings who make mistakes, have bad hair days, and aren't as funny or popular as other people we see online. And that's all okay. It really is. No one's life is as perfect as it seems online. In fact, it's the flaws and imperfections that fill this world with moments of beauty, meaning, and connection that could never be found online. We need to struggle to keep growing our strengths and realize what we're capable of. If the world was always easy and perfect, we'd never be able to do that.

Ready to practice your confidence skills? Take the 30-day challenge "My Win for the Day" on page 24, and check out "Reverse the Spotlight" on page 38.

☑ *Body Talk*

When we communicate via text with our friends and family, we lose 65 percent of what's being communicated—the nonverbal cues. It may not seem like a big deal, but it really sets us up for misinterpretations and misunderstandings.

Ada took Darron's simple "hi" response as his being uninterested or rude because she couldn't hear his tone of voice or see his body language. She also didn't know he was at work, or she wouldn't have misinterpreted the brevity of the message. I'm guessing something similar has happened to you at least once. A friend got upset when you said, "Don't worry about it," because she thought you were being dismissive, but you genuinely meant, "Please don't worry, it's not a big deal." Without tone of voice, it's important to be really clear in your text message and how it could be read. One easy way to do that is with emojis. Without going overboard, add a smiley face when you're being lighthearted or a heart when you're saying it in a loving way.

I know it's tempting to use your phone as a security blanket when you're in an awkward social situation. But with your head down and your attention on your phone, you're giving off an "I don't want to talk to you" vibe. Many students I coach tell me they're bad at making friends but then admit to being on their phone in social situations. Instead of distracting yourself with your phone, try allowing yourself to feel temporarily anxious and you might have a genuine conversation with someone who could become a potential friend in real life—and could add a few more laughs to your daily average!

Want some extra help with your body-language skills? Check out "It's Not What You Say but How You Say It" on page 74 and "Let's Face It" on page 75.

MORE ON KEEPING IT LOCKED

Is social media a happy or stressful part of your life? It's an interesting question to really ask yourself.

Given the online world is so different from the real world, it can begin to feel like you have an "online life" and an "offline life." You can filter photos and videos to the point of perfection, but they're no longer a reflection of your real life. Eventually, it begins to feel empty and stressful to feel like you always have to live up to this "image" you've created.

In my last year of high school, I used to cry myself to sleep sometimes because I felt so much self-loathing, yet every day I always had a smile on my face like I was happy and confident. No one knew what was happening beneath the surface. So please don't take anything you see online at face value. Your friend might seem super happy online, but always remember to check in on them in person. And the same goes in reverse: Never be ashamed to reach out for help if you're struggling. You don't have to put on a brave face and play pretend. We all struggle sometimes, even if we don't see that online.

Peer Pressure

"Come on, just one sip! Your parents won't even know, dude," Ren says with a laugh as he passes the vodka bottle to Eli.

"Nah, I'm alright, thanks," Eli replies, trying to sound casual and hoping Ren won't ask again. He doesn't want to look like the loser in the group, but he knows his parents would kill him if he's caught drinking, plus he really doesn't want to.

"Oh, don't be boring, Eli. You're always playing it so safe. Loosen up a little—we're only young once!"

Eli frowns a little as Ren moves across the couch and puts the bottle in his hands.

Ren knows that Eli is the only one who doesn't have a date yet for homecoming, and adds, "Anikka's coming over in like 20. She'll for sure be drinking with us and doesn't have a date. A few drinks, and I bet she'll say yes to being your homecoming date. Don't miss this just because you're a scaredy cat."

Ren leans in and pushes Eli's hand holding the bottle closer to him, just as Adan stumbles in and starts chanting, "Do it! Do it!"

The whole thing doesn't feel right to Eli. He has zero interest in drinking and has no idea how he'll hide it from his parents. But the idea of getting Anikka to go with him to homecoming sounds pretty great. "All right, let's do this!" he says with false confidence, looking at Ren and Adan, who are smirking at him.

Eli takes a massive gulp of vodka and immediately regrets it as the liquid burns, and he begins to gag. Ren and Adan are dying with laughter.

Eli takes another swig of the vodka, and he can already feel the woozy effects hitting his system. Ren and Adan egg him on, and he takes three more swigs. At some point, he passes out on the floor.

Needless to say, neither Anikka nor his parents were impressed. And there was definitely no homecoming date (or homecoming, at all). Eli was grounded for a month.

PRACTICE YOUR SKILLS

No.

Only two letters, but two of the hardest ones to say sometimes. So many of us are too caught up in pleasing people and are more worried about people liking us than us liking our own decisions. I know it's easier to "go with the flow" so you're not rejected or made fun of by a friend or someone you're trying to impress. But, in the big picture, going with the flow is the harder option because of the consequences that come with it and how it makes you feel on the other side of that choice.

Think about the last time you went along with something that didn't feel right to you. Maybe you covered for a friend with his parents. Maybe you didn't stop your friend from gossiping about another friend. At your age, your friends are everything. You're at a stage where your brain is wired to specifically seek connection and a sense of belonging with your peers. But too many of us reject who we really are to try to get people to accept who we really aren't. This will slowly eat away at you from the inside.

Think of your choices when you find yourself in a peer pressure situation:

Option 1: You choose the ease of going along with whatever they want, but on the inside, you feel ashamed of what you did—for compromising your character and what matters to you. Although you escape the temporary discomfort of being judged by others, you face the long-term discomfort of judging yourself.

Option 2: You choose the discomfort upfront and risk being rejected or teased by your friends, but on the inside, you have the long-term comfort of having your own back and living true to what matters to you. This option is kind of like pulling off the bandage—sucks for about two seconds but then it's over.

The thing is, if it's uncomfortable either way, whether you go along with them or you don't, why not choose the discomfort that keeps you living true to yourself? We only get one life; don't live yours pretending to be someone you're not.

To help you find the courage to follow through on speaking up in moments of peer pressure, I'm going to highlight some of the key social skills that come into play during these challenging situations.

☑ *Confidence and Assertiveness*

Assertiveness is absolutely key to standing up for yourself when you're being pressured by your peers. Especially the commitment to "value your values." If you believe in honesty, kindness, and hard work, and your friends ask you to do something that compromises those values, it's a straight down-the-line "no." I know it's easier said than done, but it's also not impossible. It's always possible to say no if you don't feel comfortable doing something.

Only you can set the boundaries of what you're willing to do—and not do. If it goes beyond that, you need to draw the line. You might not be able to stop others from taking action you don't like, but you can always stop yourself from participating in it.

Eli may not have been able to stop Adan and Ren from drinking, but he did have the choice to refuse the drink and leave, so he wasn't exposed to potential trouble. You may say, "But, Kate, they're my best friends! I need to do this, or they'll think I'm a loser." And I would say, "True friends never expect you to go against what matters to you." Remember the "rule of three"—Stars will never make you do something that compromises who you are. Those friends who are constantly pressuring you to do things you don't want to do may actually be Sour Worms in disguise. Be brave enough to let go of those friendships to make room in your life to find your Stars.

Want some extra strategies to build your assertiveness? Check out "Boundaries" on page 47 and "Value Your Values" on page 46, and review "The Rule of Three" on page 39.

☑ *Body Language*

So much of our communication is conveyed via nonverbal cues, which means when you're trying to stand your ground, you want to convey a confident yet calm posture that is consistent with what you're trying to tell someone. Saying no with a big smile on your face may mean they don't take you seriously. With your feet planted firmly on the ground, your arms calmly by your side, and looking directly at them, speak in a calm yet serious tone of voice.

Be careful not to launch into defense or attack mode by crossing your arms or yelling at them. That will only escalate into conflict. The goal when dealing with peer pressure is to de-escalate the tension and distance yourself from the scenario.

Even if you don't feel confident, practice 15 seconds of insane bravery. Speak calmly yet firmly with self-assured body language. Standing up for what matters to you is *always* worth it.

For some extra help with your body language, check out "Out of Your Pockets and into the Box" on page 74 and "You Don't Always Have to See Eye to Eye" on page 73.

☑ *Emotional Intelligence*

This will be a bit of a tough truth to own, but I promise I'm pointing it out from a loving place: Other people are not to blame for your actions. You are wholly responsible for how you choose to react because your actions are caused by how you think and feel about what's happening. That's on you. You can't smoke behind the school with a friend and then blame that friend when you get caught. Eli can't blame Ren and Adan for his drinking vodka and getting sick.

You always have the option to be brave, say no, and walk away. When you don't, that's on you. This isn't meant to blame you but to empower you to see that you are always in control of what you do. If at any given moment you don't like what you're doing, you can choose to change it. Or if you've already done that thing you're not proud of, you can choose to learn from it and do things differently next time. That is true empowerment in life. Remind yourself, "I always have a choice."

Want to practice your EQ? Check out "My Best Self" on page 61 and "Like a Pancake, Flip Your Complaint into a Request" on page 59.

The MORE YOU KNOW

A 2019 study by Screen Education found that 69 percent of teens wish they could spend more time hanging with their friends in person rather than online. Yet nearly 52 percent of teens admit to playing on their phones when they're hanging with their friends. So, we've got ourselves in a bit of a pickle: We wish for more time with our friends, but when we're with them, we're not even paying attention to them.

Make a pledge to change this. Say to yourself, "I promise to be mindful of putting my phone away when I'm hanging with my friends so we can enjoy meaningful conversations and fun moments together."

Isn't that the reason you are friends in the first place?

⚡ ⚡ ⚡

TAKEAWAYS

We've covered a wide range of social skills in this book, and this chapter was all about how to use these skills in a variety of ways:

- *How to be open to criticism without taking it personally.*

- *What it takes to diffuse conflict in a healthy way.*

- *Navigating the challenges of chatting with people on social media.*

- *Standing up against peer pressure so you don't compromise who you want to be in the world.*

Believe it or not, we're up to the final chapter! So, buckle up and get ready for a fun and insightful finish that ensures you're not just intellectually learning these skills, but also putting them into practice so that awkward social situations become a thing of the past!

Chapter Nine

KEEP GOING

Well, my wonderful friend, we have reached the part of the book that's just like when the pilot says, "Cabin crew, prepare the cabin for landing." It's the very final chapter before all this fun must come to an end for us. But, for you, this is just the beginning of a lifelong journey of engaging with the different ideas and strategies you've learned in this book to stop letting social awkwardness hold you back from living your best life.

USE IT OR LOSE IT

I was the captain of the tennis team during my final year of high school. I was never a standout player, but I did have a good forehand that I could smash right down the line to win the point. Recently, I got back out on the court and tried to smash the ball in the same way, and holy moly, it went flying right out of the court (and nearly hit someone in the next one—my bad!). Yes, it's safe to say I was no longer even remotely great at tennis. Why? Because I hadn't picked up a racket in eight years. I had simply stopped practicing, so all of my skills had gone down the drain. The same is true of all other skills. We either keep up our practice and commitment to get better at them, or they fade away completely.

The good news about social skills is that you will have an opportunity to practice them in nearly every area of your life. You won't have to wait for a tennis court or a racket; you simply have to walk out of your room and start chatting with one of your parents to practice active listening skills or put your hand up in class and share one of your answers to practice your self-confidence skills. The chance to practice all the strategies you've learned is everywhere. It's in the practice of using these tools that you'll transform from a highly anxious teen who rarely feels confident around others into a confident teen who only feels anxious with people *sometimes*. The key is practice. Practice equals progress!

Hone Your Skills

Let's quickly review each of the skills so I can leave you with some parting advice. Remember, I've been where you are, and I've made it to the other side.

Confidence

One thing we all do far too often is apologize, which erodes our confidence. I'm not talking about apologizing when you've genuinely done something wrong and you need to apologize. I'm talking about the "Oh, I'm sorry," you say to someone who bumps into you, or the "I'm sorry, but . . ." that you say to a friend when asking him to save you a seat.

If you were to stop and listen to how many times you apologize for yourself in a day—for things that are not even remotely close to being your fault—it would begin to make sense why you have a tendency to want to shrink away and not be seen. How you speak to yourself determines the relationship you have with yourself. By constantly saying, "Sorry," you're reinforcing the idea that other people are more important than you—even to the point of blaming yourself for their actions. It's not exactly the recipe for a healthy relationship filled with confidence.

Here's one last confidence tip I want to pass along to help you be a kind and caring human without putting yourself down all the time: Swap "I'm sorry" with "Thank you."

Instead of: "I'm sorry to be a pain, but can you please save me a seat?"

Try: "Can you please save me a seat? Thank you very much!"

By changing your apology into a "thank you," you're no longer putting yourself down at the expense of someone else. Instead, you are respecting your needs as well as appreciating the other person for accommodating you. It's a win-win!

Emotional Awareness

One thing to be mindful of when it comes to managing your emotions is to not judge yourself for not feeling happy and positive all of the time. Social media only shows the highlight reels of everyone's life, but the truth is, uncomfortable emotions are a healthy part of being human and you don't have to push them away—like trying to stuff all your dirty clothes under your bed.

There is nothing to be ashamed of if you struggle with stress or anxiety or feel frustrated sometimes. Because our thoughts create our feelings, it's simply impossible to think positively 24-7. We have a brain that's wired to keep us alive, not happy, so it needs to be very good at noticing the negative things out there in the world.

Do not layer your negative emotion with further shame and judgment. It only makes the emotion heavier and more exhausting. Instead, let it be and try out the strategy for processing uncomfortable emotions on page 26. And then when you're ready, practice PAC (see page 60) and see what other perspectives you can try on to find some relief from the uncomfortable emotion. In the meantime, please know there's no right or wrong way to feel. There just is what is.

Nonverbal Cues

A fun way to get better at picking up on nonverbal cues and also at displaying your own is as simple as muting a TV show you're watching and trying to guess the mood of the conversation without hearing what the characters are saying. It can actually be pretty entertaining to guess the attitude of each character just by watching just their eye contact and body language. Then once you've guessed how each person is feeling—whether it's angry, excited, curious, or guilty—rewind the scene to see if you're correct. If you guessed incorrectly, watch their nonverbal cues even more closely to see what you missed so that you can continue to grow your skills of interpreting nonverbal cues and properly communicating your own.

Active Listening

Active listening is one of those skills most of us *think* we're good at, but in reality, there's a lot of room for improvement. An easy way to figure out if that's the case is to ask three of the closest people in your life if they think you're a good listener. The questions can be as simple as, "Hey, do you feel like I care and understand what you say when you're talking to me? Do I help you feel heard?"

Remember, whatever their answer, don't get defensive. This is an opportunity to learn from their point of view that you can use to better yourself. You may not realize you're looking down at your hands or not providing any reaffirming feedback when someone is speaking to you. And you can't change what you're not aware of. You may think you're a great listener, but your friends and family may tell you that you always seem distracted or bored. Listen to their feedback with an open mind. Being a good listener will not only help you go further in your school pursuits and beyond, but also in your relationships.

Empathy

Shopping malls and the school bus are two amazing places to practice empathy on a daily basis because there are so many people coming and going and behaving in all sorts of ways. For example, instead of being short-tempered or frustrated with someone for getting in your way or for being rude, take a moment to stand in their shoes before you react. Remind yourself, "I have no idea what's happening in their day." Maybe they were just dumped, their dog just died, or they found out they didn't make it into college.

We may have no clue about what's happening in a stranger's day, but being empathetic may help make their day less terrible. Rather than judge your fellow shopper or passenger, see it as a chance to choose empathy and think, *Yep. I get you. This human thing is hard and sometimes I can be a jerk, too. I am going to let this go and send you good vibes.* Life just feels so much better when you do.

CUTTING TO THE CHASE

If you've reached this section of the book, it means you've been on quite the social skills journey with me! I appreciate that you've stuck with me to the end. I know your time is valuable and there are a million other important things you could be doing. But I encourage you to see that reading this book isn't time you spent but time you invested in learning some of the most valuable skills for your future.

When you walk out of your next class presentation and realize that your mind didn't go blank or that you didn't awkwardly bumble your way through small talk with friends at lunch or that you managed to start a conversation with someone new at a party, you will begin to realize why reading this book was worth it.

Human beings are social creatures, and once you know how to better connect and communicate with others, your whole world opens up. It doesn't mean you can't still enjoy time on your own or that you have to go to every party you're invited to. It means you can stop hiding from things you want to do because you're afraid of feeling anxious. This book is your guide to better managing that anxiety so you can find the courage to be more open to being social in ways that once felt too uncomfortable.

You are also the perfect age to practice these skills because your brain is primed for learning and adapting; it gives you a head start on the many adults out there who are still struggling with these social skills in their own lives. Just let yourself be a WIP (work in progress). And one day you'll look up and be proud of how far you've come.

LAST WORDS

Congratulations on reaching the very final part of this book and becoming a mini expert on all things social skills! I hope this book looks just like one of my favorite books—filled with highlights, side notes, and folded pages, earmarking my favorite parts I want to read back over later. Yes, that's right: Though our first official "road trip" together may be over, I will always be here for you.

On the days you feel ashamed for how socially awkward you are and are beating yourself up for something you said or did, pick up this book and come hang out with me. Whether it's needing to calm down after a big fight with a family member or getting a confidence boost after feeling left out at a friend's party, this book and my words will be here for you anytime.

I hope you've enjoyed reading this book as much as I've loved writing it. I'm actually getting quite emotional writing these last words because it truly has been such a gift to have the opportunity to write this book for you. This opportunity was given to me because I've worked hard at practicing everything we've learned together in this book—being more confident and more empathetic, becoming a better listener and more emotionally resilient, and being better able to connect with others in a genuine way. Those skills helped me carve the path I am now on and all the opportunities I am so grateful to have.

I am excited for the opportunities that will come your way as you continue to practice your social skills. Perhaps a new friendship that brings a lifetime of memories? A new summer job that sets you on track for your career? A healthier relationship with your siblings that makes being at home way more fun? Or a chance at being team captain, winning a part in the musical, or being elected to student council? Whatever the opportunity, there's only one way to find out what it could be—get to practicing these skills! Every day is a perfect day to practice.

Resources

Further Reading

Beyond this book, there are tons of great resources at your fingertips to continue to help you grow your skills and become more confident at communicating with anyone. Here are some of my personal favorites that I recommend you check out.

To learn more about building social skills specifically, you can check out these awesome books:

Bocci, Goali Saedi. *The Social Media Workbook for Teens: Skills to Help You Balance Screen Time, Manage Stress & Take Charge of Your Life*. Oakland, CA: Instant Help Books, 2019.

Cain, Susan, Gregory Mone, Erica Moroz, and Grant Snider. *Quiet Power: The Secret Strengths of Introverts*. New York: Dial Books, 2016.

Cooper, Barbara and Nancy Widdows. *The Social Success Workbook for Teens: Skill-Building Activities for Teens with Nonverbal Learning Disorder, Asperger's Disorder, and Other Social-Skill Problems*. Oakland, CA: Instant Help Books, 2008.

Goulston, Mark. *Just Listen: Discover the Secret to Getting Through to Absolutely Anyone*. New York: AMACOM, 2010.

MacLeod, Chris. *The Social Skills Guidebook: Manage Shyness, Improve Your Conversations, and Make Friends, Without Giving Up Who You Are*. Ontario: Chris MacLeod, 2016.

Reagan, Laura Lyles. *How to Raise Respectful Parents: Better Communication for Teen and Parent Relationships*. Abbeville, SC: Moonshine Cove Publishing, 2016.

Van Dijk, Sheri. *Relationship Skills 101 for Teens: Your Guide to Dealing with Daily Drama, Stress & Difficult Emotions Using DBT*. Oakland, CA: New Harbinger Publications, 2015.

Here are some of my favorite self-help books that aren't specifically about communication, but dive deeper into a specific social skill that we've touched on in this book:

Great to help you build a growth mindset and for self-motivation: Dweck, Dr. Carol S. *Mindset: Changing the Way You Think to Fulfil Your Potential*. London: Robinson, 2012.

Amazing for self-confidence tips: Brown, Brené. *The Gifts of Imperfection: Let Go of Who You Think You're Supposed to Be and Embrace Who You Are*. Center City, MN: Hazelden Publishing, 2010.

To help you build emotional intelligence and better manage your thoughts: Edelman, Sarah and Louise Rémond. *Good Thinking: A Teenager's Guide to Managing Stress and Emotion Using CBT*. Jacksonville, FL: ABC Books, 2017.

An all-around amazing story by a Holocaust survivor who truly opens your eyes to the power of empathy: Jaku, Eddie. *The Happiest Man on Earth*. Sydney: Macmillan Australia, 2020.

Social Media

There are also some wonderful coaches on Instagram with inspiring and practical content to help you keep building up your social skills, including:

Amy Koch, Anxiety/Confidence Coach for Teens & Parents *@amykoch.findyourmind*

Kate Fitzsimons, International Resilience Speaker and Certified LCS Life Coach *for Teens @katemaree_fitz*

KnowingUP: Teen Life Coaching, Certified LCS Life Coach *@thelifecoachforteengirls*

Teen Ideas Matter (Community) *@teenideasmatter*

Further Listening

Prefer to listen to something rather than read it? I got you! Here are some awesome podcasts that are specifically for teens and will keep teaching you strategies to build your self-confidence and social skills.

Okay. Now What?! with Kate Fitzsimons—Yes, yours truly! I have my own podcast and would love for you to keep listening and learning along with me! I especially think you'll love Episode 89, "Social Anxiety and Being Less Awkward Meeting People."

Secrets for an Awesome Life with Joey Mascio

The Teen Life Coach with guest host Sami Halvorsen

Apps

Here are two meditation apps for both Apple and Android platforms that I personally use and recommend:

Calm: Guided meditations, sleep stories, breathing programs, and relaxing music

Insight Timer: Guided meditations and talks by meditation and mindfulness experts, psychologists, and teachers

References

Advaney, Martina. "To Talk or Not to Talk That Is the Question!" *YouthTime Magazine*. May 6, 2017. Youth-Time.eu/to-talk-or-not -to-talk-that-is-the-question-at-least-70-percent-of-communication -is-non-verbal.

Brody, Jane E. "Social Interaction Is Critical for Mental and Physical Health." *New York Times*. June 12, 2017. Accessed July 8, 2020. NYTimes.com/2017/06/12/well/live/having-friends-is-good-for -you.html.

Center for Healthy Minds. "5 Tips for Empathy-Building in Youth." Accessed August 23, 2020. CenterHealthyMinds.org/join-the -movement/5-tips-for-empathy-building-in-teens.

Center for Parent & Teen Communication. "8 Strategies to Handle Peer Pressure." January 25, 2019. Accessed September 10, 2020. ParentAndTeen.com/say-no-peer-pressure.

Cherry, Kendra. "What Is the Negativity Bias?" Verywell Mind. April 29, 2020. Accessed October 13, 2020. VerywellMind.com /negative-bias-4589618.

Chesak, Jennifer. "Social Media Is Killing Your Friendships." Healthline. September 18, 2018. Accessed July 20, 2020. Healthline.com /health/how-social-media-is-ruining-relationships.

The Coaching Tools Company. "THINK Acronym for Kinder and More Effective Communications (Infographic)." February 24, 2016. Accessed September 10, 2020. TheCoachingTools Company.com/think-acronym-for-kinder-and-more-effective -communications.

Cohut, Maria. "What Are the Benefits of Being Social?" Medical News Today. February 23, 2018. Accessed October 13, 2020. MedicalNewsToday.com/articles/321019#face-to-face-contact -is-like-a-vaccine.

Common Sense Media. "The Common Sense Census: Media Use by Tweens and Teens." Accessed October 13, 2020. Common SenseMedia.org/sites/default/files/uploads/research/census _researchreport.pdf.

Connelly, Mark. "Social Awareness." Change Management Coach. Updated September 12, 2020. Accessed October 12, 2020. Change -Management-Coach.com/social-awareness.html.

Cuncic, Arlin. "How to Overcome Eye Contact Anxiety." Verywell Mind. Updated December 5, 2019. Accessed August 18, 2020. VerywellMind.com/how-do-i-maintain-good-eye-contact-3024392.

Dewar, Gwen. "The Case for Teaching Empathy." Parenting Science. Accessed August 23, 2020. ParentingScience.com/teaching -empathy.html.

Dodgson, Lindsay. "Your DNA Determines Whether You're an Introvert or an Extrovert—Here's How to Tell Which One You Are." *Business Insider Australia.* April 20, 2018. Accessed July 10, 2020. BusinessIn- sider.com.au/why-people-are-extroverts-or-introverts -2018-4?r=US&IR=T.

Economy, Peter. "This Is the Way You Need to Write Down Your Goals for Faster Success." *INC.* Accessed July 20, 2020. Inc.com /peter-economy/this-is-way-you-need-to-write-down-your-goals -for-faster-success.html.

Fuller, J. Ryan. "The Impact of Social Media on Social Skills." New York Behavioral Health. Accessed September 8, 2020. NewYork BehavioralHealth.com/the-impact-of-social-media-use-on -social-skills.

Georgiev, Deyan. "51+ Scary Smartphone Addiction Statistics for 2020 [Nomophobia on the Rise]." *Tech Jury* (blog). July 2, 2020. Accessed September 8, 2020. TechJury.net/blog/smartphone -addiction-statistics/#gref.

Goodreads. "Ambrose of Milan > Quotes > Quotable Quote." Accessed October 12, 2020. Goodreads.com/quotes/801696-no-one-heals -himself-by-wounding-another.

Goodreads. "Dita Von Teese > Quotes> Quotable Quote." Accessed October 12, 2020. Goodreads.com/quotes/628953-you-can-be -the-ripest-juiciest-peach-in-the-world.

Goodreads. "E. H. Mayo > Quotes > Quotable Quote." Accessed October 12, 2020. Goodreads.com/quotes/7683591-one-friend -one-person-who-is-truly-understanding-who-takes.

Goodreads. "H. Jackson Brown Jr. > Quotes > Quotable Quote." Accessed October 12, 2020. Goodreads.com/quotes/41423 -remember-that-everyone-you-meet-is-afraid-of-something -loves.

Goodreads. "Seneca the Younger Essays Volume 1 Quotes." Accessed October 12, 2020. Goodreads.com/work/quotes/68267943-seneca -the-younger-essays-volume-1.

Grohol, John M. "Become a Better Listener: Active Listening." PsychCentral. Updated May 20, 2020. Accessed August 22, 2020. PsychCentral.com/lib/become-a-better-listener-active-listening.

Hall, Jeffrey A. "How Many Hours Does It Take to Make a Friend?" *Journal of Social and Personal Relationships* 36, no. 4 (March 2018): 1278–1296. doi.org/10.1177/0265407518761225.

Ignite Treatment Centers. "Social Media and Social Anxiety in Teenagers." Accessed September 12, 2020. IgniteTeenTreatment .com/social-media-social-anxiety-teenagers.

The India Economic Times. "Turns Out, Being Shy or a Social Butterfly Depends on Your Genes." August 28, 2017. Accessed July 16, 2020. EconomicTimes.IndiaTimes.com/magazines/panache/turns-out

-being-shy-or-a-social-butterfly-depends-on-yourgenes/articleshow
/60260636.cms.

Khush, Harwant. "Boost Nonverbal Communication Skills for
Success." Tero International, Inc. Accessed August 9, 2020.
Tero.com/articles/boost-nonverbal-communication-skills.php.

Kid Sense Child Development. "Social Skills." Accessed October 13,
2020. ChildDevelopment.com.au/areas-of-concern/play-and
-social-skills/social-skills.

Konrath, Sara, Edward H. O'Brien, and Courtney Hsing. "Changes in
Dispositional Empathy in American College Students Over Time: A
Meta-Analysis." *Personality and Social Psychology Review* 15, no. 2
(August 2010): 180–198. doi.org/10.1177/1088868310377395.

Lenhart, Amanda. "Teens, Technology and Friendships: Video Games,
Social Media and Mobile Phones Play an Integral Role in How Teens
Meet and Interact with Friends." Pew Research Center. August 6,
2015. Accessed October 14, 2020. PewResearch
.org/internet/2015/08/06/teens-technology-and-friendships.

Luna, Kaitlin. "Dealing with Digital Distraction." American
Psychological Association. August 10, 2018. Accessed October 13,
2020. APA.org/news/press/releases/2018/08/digital-distraction.aspx.

Mackay, Bea. "Communication Skill 8: Reflective Listening." *Bea
in Balance* (blog). March 14, 2013. Accessed August 22, 2020.
BeaInBalance.com/relationship-communication-skills-reflect
-it-back.

MacLeod, Chris. "Why Even Be More Social in the First Place?"
Succeed Socially. Accessed July 11, 2020. SucceedSocially.com
/whybesocial.

Melbourne Child Psychology & School Psychology Services. "How
to Help Teenagers Develop Empathy." Accessed August 23, 2020.
MelbourneChildPsychology.com.au/blog/help-teenagers
-develop-empathy.

Moore, Catherine. "Teaching Emotional Intelligence to Teens and Students." Positive Psychology. Updated September 1, 2020. Accessed October 12, 2020. PositivePsychology.com/teaching -emotional-intelligence.

Morin, Amy. "How Assertiveness Improves Communication Skills." Verywell Family. Updated June 11, 2020. Accessed July 31, 2020. VerywellFamily.com/ways-assertiveness-skills-help-teens -2610996.

Mosley, Tonya, and Serena McMahon. "Social Media Use Linked to Anxiety, Depression among Teens, New Study Finds." WBUR. January 9, 2020. Accessed September 12, 2020. WBUR.org/hereandnow/2020/01/09/social-media-anxiety -depression-teens.

Navarro, Joe. "Body Language Essentials for Your Children—for Parents." *Psychology Today*. April 9, 2010. Accessed August 8, 2020. PsychologyToday.com/au/blog/spycatcher/201004 /body-language-essentials-your-children-parents.

The Nemours Foundation. "Assertiveness." KidsHealth.org. Accessed July 31, 2020. KidsHealth.org/en/teens/assertive.

The Nemours Foundation. "Emotional Intelligence." KidsHealth.org. Accessed August 7, 2020. KidsHealth.org/en/teens/eq.

Newport Academy. "The Importance of Teen Friendship." July 2, 2018. Accessed July 12, 2020. NewportAcademy.com/resources /empowering-teens/teen-friendships.

New World Encyclopedia. "Society." Accessed August 6, 2020. NewWorldEncyclopedia.org/entry/society.

Oxford Learning. "Tips & Activities to Improve Your Child's Active Listening Skills." June 13, 2017. Accessed August 22, 2020. Oxford-Learning.com/improve-active-listening-skills.

Paradigm Treatment. "7 Ways to Teach Teens Emotional Intelligence." May 12, 2017. Accessed August 7, 2020. ParadigmTreatment.com /7-teach-teens-emotional-intelligence.

ReachOut Australia. "Raising an Emotionally Intelligent Child." Accessed August 8, 2020. Parents.AU.ReachOut.com/skills-to -build/connecting-and-communicating/things-to-try-supportive -parenting/help-your-teenager-develop-emotional-intelligence.

Sandoiu, Ana. "Strong Friendships in Adolescence May Benefit Mental Health in the Long Run." Medical News Today. August 26, 2017. Accessed July 11, 2020. MedicalNewsToday.com/articles/319119.

Schulz, Jodie. "Eye Contact: Don't Make These Mistakes." Michigan State University Extension. December 31, 2012. Accessed August 18, 2020. CANR.MSU.edu/news/eye_contact_dont _make_these_mistakes.

Schulze, Lars, Babette Renneberg, and Janek S. Lobmaier. "Gaze Perception in Social Anxiety and Social Anxiety Disorder." *Frontiers in Human Neuroscience* 7 (December 2013): 872. doi.org/10.3389/fnhum.2013.00872.

Screen Education. "Teen Smartphone Addiction National Survey 2018." Accessed October 14, 2020. ScreenEducation.org/uploads /1/1/6/6/116602217/teen_smartphone_addiction_national _survey_2018_report_6.21.18_upload_version_1.2.pdf.

Shellenbarger, Sue. "Teenagers Are Still Developing Empathy Skills." *Wall Street Journal.* October 15, 2013. Accessed August 24, 2020. WSJ.com/articles/teens-are-still-developing-empathy-skills -1381876015.

Shultz, David. "Video: How Long Can You Make Eye Contact before Things Start to Get Uncomfortable?" *Science.* July 5, 2016. Accessed October 13, 2020. ScienceMag.org/news/2016/07 /video-how-long-can-you-make-eye-contact-things-start-get -uncomfortable?utm_source=newsfromscience&utm_medium =twitter&utm_campaign=eyecontact-5509.

SmartSocial.com. "Teen Social Media Statistics 2020 (What Parents Need to Know)." February 25, 2020. Accessed July 20, 2020. SmartSocial.com/social-media-statistics.

Sólo, Andre. "Are You Born an Introvert, or Do You Become One?" Introvert, Dear. March 14, 2016. Accessed July 8, 2020. IntrovertDear.com/news/are-you-born-an-introvert-or-do -you-become-one.

Srigley, Ron. "I Asked My Students to Turn in Their Cell Phones and Write about Living without Them." *MIT Technology Review*. December 26, 2019. Accessed September 8, 2020. TechnologyReview.com/2019/12/26/131179/teenagers -without-cell-phones.

Stony Brook University. "Sensitive? Emotional? Empathetic? It Could Be in Your Genes." ScienceDaily. June 23, 2014. Accessed August 28, 2002. ScienceDaily.com/releases/2014/06 /140623091828.htm.

Torres, Monica. "Science Tells Us How Long It Takes an Adult to Make a New Friend." Ladders. April 11, 2018. Accessed August 18, 2020. TheLadders.com/career-advice/science-tells-us-how-long -it-takes-an-adult-to-make-friends.

Van Edwards, Vanessa. "20 Hand Gestures You Should Be Using and Their Meaning." ScienceOfPeople.com. Accessed August 18, 2020. ScienceOfPeople.com/hand-gestures.

Vice President for Communications, University of Michigan. "Empathy: College Students Don't Have as Much as They Used To." Michigan News. May 27, 2010. News.UMich.edu/empathy -college-students-don-t-have-as-much-as-they-used-to.

Index

Acknowledgments

I am forever grateful to Callisto Media for the opportunity to publish this book—most especially to Joe Cho for being the spark that made this happen and Meera Pal for guiding me through this whole process with such enthusiasm.

To my wonderful fiancé, Nate, thank you for being patient on my long writing days and for lifting me up with your inspiring words when I needed it most.

I'd love to also acknowledge my amazing family for their endless belief in me and especially my sister, Nicole, for being my inspiration to leave this world better than I found it—just like she did. I truly hope this book becomes part of that legacy for us both.

About the Author

Kate Fitzsimons is an international youth speaker, certified life coach, and teen resilience specialist. From a brokenhearted sister battling an eating disorder to one of Australia's "100 Women of Influence," Kate is living proof that what doesn't kill us can make us stronger.

Through her school talks, online coaching, and podcast *Okay. Now What?!* Kate has shared her empowering message with more than 200,000 students to help them overcome any adversity they face. Her passion to make a difference for youth has seen her featured alongside professional surfer Kelly Slater on Arianna Huffington's Thrive Global website and named as one of Tourism Fiji's "Bulanaires"—a title that celebrates those rich in positivity and resilience.

Originally from Sydney, Australia, Kate now lives happily with her fiancé in Princeton, New Jersey. Her favorite things include RubySnap cookies and long walks with her dog, Jaku.

For more information about Kate, visit KateFitzsimons.com or connect with her online:

Instagram: @katemaree_fitz
Facebook: Facebook.com/fitzsimonskate
LinkedIn: LinkedIn.com/in/fitzsimonskate